THEORY AND TRUTH

Theory and Truth

Philosophical Critique
within Foundational Science

LAWRENCE SKLAR

OXFORD
UNIVERSITY PRESS

OXFORD

UNIVERSITY PRESS

Great Clarendon Street, Oxford OX2 6DP

Oxford University Press is a department of the University of Oxford
It furthers the University's objective of excellence in research, scholarship,
and education by publishing worldwide in

Oxford New York

Athens Auckland Bangkok Bogotá Buenos Aires Calcutta
Cape Town Chennai Dar es Salaam Delhi Florence Hong Kong Istanbul
Karachi Kuala Lumpur Madrid Melbourne Mexico City Mumbai
Nairobi Paris São Paulo Singapore Taipei Tokyo Toronto Warsaw

with associated companies in Berlin Ibadan

Oxford is a registered trade mark of Oxford University Press
in the UK and in certain other countries

Published in the United States
by Oxford University Press Inc., New York

British Library Cataloguing in Publication Data

Data available

Library of Congress Cataloging in Publication Data

xx

ISBN 0-19-823849-5

1 3 5 7 9 10 8 6 4 2

Typeset by Invisible Ink
Printed in Great Britain
on acid-free paper by
Biddles Ltd
Guildford & King's Lynn

To the Memory of Peter Hempel

ACKNOWLEDGMENTS

The material in these essays was originally presented in the form of six talks given as the John Locke Lectures at Oxford University during the Trinity term of the 1997–8 academic year. I am deeply grateful to Oxford University and to the Faculty of Litterae Humaniores and the Sub-Faculty of Philosophy for inviting me to Oxford and giving me the opportunity to present the lectures. I would also like to thank the Fellows of All Souls College for the support and warm hospitality they provided me as a Visiting Fellow at All Souls for the term of the lectures.

I am also very grateful for the support provided by the National Endowment for the Humanities in the form of a Fellowship for University Teachers for the academic year 1995–6. This fellowship aided in the provision of released time during which the initial research leading to these essays was undertaken. I am greatly indebted to the National Science Foundation which provided me with support for three summer periods of research that allowed the material of these essays to be further developed and brought into their current publishable form. This support is also providing an opportunity for me to continue research in the directions outlined in these essays in order that some topics treated briefly here may be developed in a more extended form.

I am also grateful to the University of Michigan whose support for a sabbatical year supplemented the grant from the National Endowment for the Humanities.

I wish to express my special gratitude to Simon Saunders, Harvey Brown, Jeremy Butterfield, and Orly Shenker at Oxford, and to Jamie Tappenden, Marc Kelly, James Woodbridge, Peter Vranas, Richard Schoonhoven, and Gerhard Nuffer at Michigan for their helpful discussions about and comments on the material of these essays. Thanks are also due to my colleagues David Hills and James Joyce for the help with the Suggested Readings, and to Angela Blackburn for her great help in bringing the manuscript of the book into readable form.

L.S.

CONTENTS

Introduction

The core purpose of these essays is to argue that there are a number of issues in the methodology of science that have not received the attention they deserve. Focusing on these issues from a methodological standpoint will, I argue, at the same time bring together in a novel way a number of well-known problems that arise in the philosophical discussion of foundational issues that are concerned with the specific problems of fundamental theories in physics. The book, then, is simultaneously concerned with philosophy of science as methodology and philosophy of science as philosophy of physics.

The overall theme is that there are ways of thinking that are used in abstract philosophy, and in philosophical methodology of science, that make their appearance *within* the practice of fundamental science itself. It is then argued that when these philosophical themes appear within the development and critique of fundamental theory within science, they take on a very different aspect from how they appear in more abstract methodological practice.

Specifically, the argument focuses on several reasons that have been offered in general philosophy and methodological philosophy of science for being skeptical of any claims to truth being made for foundational theories in science. The essays are designed to show that critical exploration of foundational theories based upon grounds that are familiar from the general methodology can be found as essential, internal parts of scientific practice, when that practice is directed to the discovery, refinement, and revision of foundational theories.

Making this overall point requires paying attention to a wide range of philosophical work directed at the kinds of skepticism that appear in general methodology. But it also requires directing attention to a large number of discussions of specific issues within the foundations of physics that are concerned with specific difficulties with specific foundational theories. For it is primarily by displaying a wide range of important examples of the role played by critical philosophical methods within science that the main points will be made. It is these examples that will illustrate the main themes that philosophical modes of reasoning appear within science itself, but that when they do they take on a structure quite different in important ways from the structure they have when they are employed in general methodology.

The scope of this book is, then, quite broad, touching as it does both on a wide spectrum of traditional issues in general philosophy and the general methodology of science, and on a wide range of issues from the philosophical foundations of physics. The book, though, is quite short. This is deliberate, as the intention of these essays, like that of the lectures from which they are derived, is to direct attention to a very wide range of problems that can gain clarity by being seen as component issues in a systematic scheme of a way of doing the philosophy of science. My hope is that looking at the problems in this somewhat novel way will direct further attention to the exploration of each individual problem at the length and in the detail that it deserves.

Not surprisingly, then, the issues discussed here are treated in quite a broad-brush fashion. Material worthy of intensive and extended discussion is often covered in only a brief paragraph or two. This is the price that has to be paid if one is to compress a very wide range of issues into a brief treatment of the overall theme.

In partial compensation for this inevitable brevity and sketchiness, I have appended to each of the first four chapters a brief, annotated, "Suggested Readings" section. Here the reader is directed both to a number of works in general methodology of science, and to works in foundational physics and its philosophical study, works that can be profitably studied by someone who wants to fill in the many details that are skimmed over in the body of the text of these essays. These reading suggestions are by no means intended to provide even the beginnings of an exhaustive bibliography on the subjects in question, but only to provide the reader with initial access to the literature on the issues of philosophy or physics in question.

I

Theory and Truth

Arguments abound to the effect that we ought to deny claims to the truth of even our best, most widely accepted scientific theories. Some of these skeptical arguments would have us believe that we ought to deny any representational validity to our scientific theories at all, or, at least, that we ought to forgo claiming any kind of epistemic warrant for taking them as representative of the nature of the world in any sense. I will not be concerned with such wildly radical skepticisms here.

Some more modest brands of skepticism have held, rather, that although we can in some sense legitimately assert the representational power of our best available science, we ought to eschew any claim to its uniqueness as the best account of the world. Many of the varieties of currently trendy relativisms seem to be trying to convince us of that.

But it is not that set of reasons for denying that our best theories are true that I will be dealing with, either. The science I will be concentrating my attention on is fundamental physics. Some relativizing views emphasize the dependence of the scientific world-view adopted on various cultural or social conditions in which the scientist is, usually unconsciously, embedded. Whatever the plausibility may be that our social embodiment makes any kind of objective history or social science unlikely, difficult, or even impossible, that such theories as Newtonian mechanics, special and general relativity, statistical mechanics, or quantum mechanics are replete with presumptions that do little more than express concealed ideology, or that they could and would be replaced by some radically different alternative having equally good claims to represent the physical world were our social matrix different than it is, is an idea that is as dubious as it is currently popular. My concern here will not, however, be with such things as Lenard's "German (as opposed to Jewish) physics," with "Marxist physics based on dialectical materialism," or with any of the current fashionable versions of alleged cultural relativity in science.

There are other, more modest, relativisms that would argue from the openness of our inference from experiment to theory, and from the internal social dynamics of practicing science, to elements of hidden contingency in our theory choice. These more moderate relativistic claims are certainly more plausible, and more interesting, than those of radical social constructivists. But it is not this kind of "internal relativism" that I will be focusing my attention on, either. Some of the matters with which I will deal, though, have played a role in one or another of such relativistic claims.

On the other hand, I will certainly not be arguing that no plausible case can be made for the claim that some parts of some of our very best fundamental physical theories of the world may be subject to allegations of arbitrariness or conventionality. But any arguments for the kinds of arbitrariness with which I will be concerned have their grounding in matters quite distinct from any claims about the socially constructed nature of science, whether those claims are grandly externalist or modestly internalist.

Let me begin by noting very briefly three kinds of reasons why we might want to claim that we ought not to think of our fundamental physical theories as giving us true representations of the world, and, as a consequence, that we ought to refrain from asserting them as correct in any straightforward sense.

First, there are those doubts about the representational nature of our theories that arise from skepticism concerning the legitimacy of positing unobservable entities and properties in explanation of the observable phenomena upon which our postulation of those theories rests as evidence.

The history of these skepticisms concerning the unobservable is a long one. Criticisms of then current physical theories that rest upon skeptical doubts about their ontological posits in the realm of the unobservable can be found in ancient Greek astronomy, that is, in the claims that the aim of astronomy was to "save the observable phenomena," and not to posit physical explanations of them in the form of crystalline spheres and the like. Similar critiques of theory as illegitimately positing the unobservable can be found in the nineteenth-century attack on atomism by energeticists such as Mach and Duhem. As we shall see, the rejection of the unobservable takes on many forms in contemporary fundamental physics.

The core idea here, in its weaker version, is that insofar as we posit a realm of the unobservable, we reach beyond the realm of evidential legitimacy that rests on the support of theories by observationally accessible experiment. In its stronger version the claim is that assertions about the unobservable are semantically unintelligible. In many of its versions this way of thinking leads either to proposals to reformulate the theory in such a way that it makes no reference to unobservables at all, or, alternatively, to keep the theory as it stands but refrain from fully asserting it or fully believing it to be true. Instead, the latter approach goes, we ought to think of ourselves as only asserting the instrumental adequacy of the theory or believing it as an "as-if" fictionalist account whose real purpose is merely the economical summary of the observable phenomena it predicts.

Next, there are those doubts about the simple truth of our theories that rest upon the observation that fundamental physical theory is applicable to systems in the real world only after numerous crucial idealizations have been made.

It is observed that no real physical system in the world is ever such that our theories can directly, and without qualification, deal with it in a predictive or explanatory way. Our theories, for example, deal only with limited classes of causal influences on a system, but real systems are subject to an infinitude of disturbing influences, known and unknown. Further, our theories deal only with specific and limited aspects of a system, but real systems have multitudes of interacting features that cannot be taken account of in any single physical characterization. Finally, in many cases our theories only apply to systems when they are idealized in some respect or other, say, as being limitingly small or limitingly large, or when their behavior is dealt with only in some idealized way, say, over times in the limit of zero time intervals or in the limit of infinite time intervals. But the real behavior of real systems as we experimentally observe it is never the idealized behavior of such idealized systems as the theory is strictly capable of encompassing.

We ought not, then, it is argued, think of our theories as really true of the world. Perhaps we can find some other general semantic relation our scientific assertions can legitimately bear to the systems to which they are applied. Or, perhaps, we can retain our simple semantic relations by denying that the scientific assertions are intended to be about real systems at all. Perhaps we can hold them to be assertible only of "models," considered as abstractions from the world. We might then construct some appropriate "similarity" relation of model to real system that will mediate the relationship of scientific claim to real world.

Finally, there are those doubts about the simple truth of our theories that rest upon our awareness that even our very best current fundamental physical theories are unlikely to survive as permanently accepted best theories in the ongoing evolution of science into the future.

We do not believe that the future scientific community will accept our currently best fundamental physical theories as the theories they will espouse. We believe that our theories have, at most, a transient role as top contenders in the contest of hypotheses with one another. Like modern fame, scientific acceptability lasts but fifteen minutes. There are many reasons why we believe that our current theories will eventually, perhaps soon, be rejected. They fail to fit the full range of experimental facts, that is, they are afflicted with empirical anomalies. They have internal structural features that we find unacceptable, internal formal inconsistencies, for example. They often contradict other best available theories, leading us to believe that at least some of our current theories cannot be the last word. Finally, we have the overriding experience from past science that even the most deeply cherished fundamental theories of one generation are usually rejected as outmoded failures by succeeding generations of scientists.

How, then, could we possibly think of claiming that our current best theories are true to the world? Once again, must we not think of some other way of describing the relation of our current theories to the world that is subtler than saying that the theory is correct or true to the world? After all, it hardly seems rational to simultaneously assert the theory to be correct and at the same time to believe that in the future it will quite reasonably be rejected as one more failed theory that transiently occupied the position of "best available theory to date."

I am deeply sympathetic to each of these kinds of doubt. The interpretive issues raised by the problem of the unobservable ontology of theories, by the theories being applicable only in an idealized context, and by the theories' assumed transience in the history of ever-changing theories, are real issues. Nor would I want to deny that insights can be obtained by exploring these issues in a manner that is highly abstracted from the specific theories encountered in fundamental physics.

But exploration at this abstract level is precisely what I do not wish to pursue here. I do not intend to enter deeply into the debates about these issues that are profitably being carried out at a purely philosophical level, that is, in a manner which does everything in its power to abstract from the specifics of contemporary scientific theories and which uses examples from such theories merely as illustrative cases to illuminate abstractly obtained results.

What I want to do here, rather, is to make a kind of meta-philosophical claim and to support it with some very briefly surveyed case studies. I will argue that there is a way to explore the issues noted above which is, perhaps, more replete with interesting philosophical problems than those encountered when they are dealt with in grand philosophical abstraction, or when the specifics of the scientific theories play at best the role of illustrative examples of general, abstract theses. I will explore the way in which the three critical aspects of theories—their reference to an unobservable ontology, their resort to systematic idealization, and their transient status—all make their appearance *within* the scientific context of the framing, testing, adjudicating, and revising of theories within foundational physics itself. I will argue that various kinds of reasoning that we normally think of as philosophical are deeply embedded in the very practice of science. This embedding of philosophy in science can be clearly seen only when one explores in some detail the ways in which empirical data, hypothesis formation, and philosophical critique all interact in the body of science itself.

I will claim that by exploring such issues as ontological elimination grounded in empiricist critique, the critical exploration of the relationship between a science treating of ideals and the real systems under study, and the critical understanding of our current theories as mere way-stations in an ongoing and changing science, and by exploring these issues as they function within science itself, we can discover a rich structure of philosophically interesting methodological, epistemological, and metaphysical topics whose very existence might not be realized by someone approaching the problems in a too broad and abstract manner. When the three critical aspects of theories are looked at within the context of the generation, testing, and criticism of specific theories in foundational physics, many of the key issues that arise turn out to be quite different from those that have attracted attention when those same three critical aspects have been dealt with in the usual abstract fashion.

By pursuing this project I hope also to cast doubt on any idea that methodological philosophy of science can be carried on above the fray of the specific issues and debates that arise in the scientific treatment of our best available foundational physical theories. At the same time I would like to challenge any idea that scientific practice is sufficiently independent of philosophy that we can take a "quietist" attitude toward fundamental scientific theories, taking them as givens that are in no way in need of philosophical interpretation or critique. That is because, as I shall argue, philosophical critique is part and parcel of their very nature as scientific theories. In other words, I will argue for the inextricability of science and philosophy.

I will also be concerned with making a few tentative speculations about what might be the relationship between the consideration of the three critical aspects in the usual abstract way and the consideration of them in the more contextual and theory-specific way to be emphasized here. I will suggest that the global philosophical questions and the answers proposed to them may themselves stand to the more local issues as some form of limiting ideal. This observation may provide some useful insights into how to think about the global problems in their own right.

I will, then, work at a level that is intermediate between the philosophical approach that attempts to abstract completely from the specifics of the physical theories, and the philosophy-of-physics approach that treats philosophical issues only as they appear within the context of very specific physical theories. My hope is that working at this level we shall find many common elements in critical examinations of quite distinct physical theories, but shall still see each issue in the context of a specific scientific theory, in abstraction from which it cannot profitably be discussed.

Working in this way, and trying to make these claims plausible, will require, of course, outlining a number of specific examples of how philosophical modes of reasoning function in scientific debates and in theory constructions and reconstructions in physics. Dealing with any one of these examples in anything remotely like the detail it deserves will be impossible here. I am arguing that the specific details of physical science, empirical and conceptual, must be attended to exhaustively and with care if we are really to understand how any of the critical philosophical themes show up in science itself. But in this book I clearly cannot hope to deal with the notoriously complex and difficult foundational problems in relativistic spacetime theories, statistical mechanics, quantum mechanics, or quantum field theory.

I must then ask for the reader's patience and generosity when, as will be necessary, I touch briefly, and, alas, superficially, on the outlines of some of the major problem areas of the philosophy of physics. I will try to provide enough detail in a non-technical manner to explain how the examples chosen illustrate the philosophical morals I am trying to draw. But I will certainly not be able here to provide anything remotely resembling a serious in-depth treatment of any one of the specific issues in the foundations of physics. Nor will I be able to provide extensive and conclusive arguments to the effect that the examples used truly support my general theses. My aim is to promote a way of doing the philosophy of science that, while not unknown, is, perhaps, not practiced enough. Here I cannot carry out any of the proposed philosophical explorations in any seriousness, but can only suggest what kinds of problematics appear in this area and hint at some of the ways in which the kinds of problems that do arise might be approached.

Suggested Readings

In the program casting doubt on the naive idea that scientific theories express the unique truth about the world, a central text that rests on the claim of science as culturally relative is Bloor (1991). An argument for the relativity of science founded on internal aspects of scientific method is Pickering (1984). For a sophisticated version of "deeper" philosophical motivations for perspectivalist views about science, coming from the tradition of Kant, German idealism, and pragmatism, see Putnam (1978) and Putnam (1990). For doubts about scientific truth founded on science's need to idealize see Cartwright (1983). Two classics that emphasize the radical transience of science and infer from that profound philosophical consequences are Kuhn (1970) and Feyerabend (1962).

2

Ontological Elimination

1. ONTOLOGICAL ELIMINATION FOUNDED ON CRITIQUE

Both philosophers and scientists frequently tell us that what we had supposed to exist really does not exist. In our explorations in this book about the scientific rejection of some kind of putative furniture of the world, we are not concerned with every kind of rejection that comes about because one theory is replaced by some successor that rejects a portion of the old theory's posits. We are not concerned, for example, with such cases as the denial that there are crystalline spheres or that there are such substances as caloric or phlogiston. We are concerned, rather, with cases where rejecting a portion of the ontology is motivated by the idea that an existing theory can be reinterpreted in such a way as to eliminate it as being unnecessary to the theory's real purposes, thereby resulting in an improved version of the existing theory. We are also concerned with those cases where the older theory is, indeed, replaced by some alternative newer theory, but where the replacement itself has such an ontologically reductive interpretive move as a crucial part of its motivation.

The kind of philosophical ontological elimination I have in mind is not that suggested by programs of wholesale and global elimination of all or a substantial part of the theoretical ontology of the world, such as the reinterpretive accounts of theories given by radical positivism, instrumentalism, or phenomenalism. In these philosophical cases of the elimination of ontology it is transparent from the start that the arguments in favor of the eliminativist programs are founded on epistemological considerations. Basic to such claims has always been the epistemological assertion that the entities in question are outside the grasp of proper evidential warrant and, hence, that either we have no grounds for accepting statements about them into our corpus of belief, or, more strongly, that such statements are devoid of cognitive significance altogether.

Such epistemological concerns play a fundamental role in the scientific eliminativist programs I will be focusing on here as well, as we shall see. But it is the cases of reinterpretation of theories by ontological elimination that go on within science, in all their local and contextual nature, that I want to pay attention to, and not the global philosophical reinterpretive programs.

Let me begin by simply noting a number of themes I will try to develop shortly.

(1) Eliminative reinterpretation of theory as it functions within foundational physics is always motivated by special features of the experimental and theoretical situation at the time the reinterpretation takes place. It is never motivated solely by general epistemological principles of an empiricist or positivist kind.

(2) Nevertheless, each such reinterpretation invokes just the sort of epistemologically motivated arguments that are familiar from the global, philosophical programs. These arguments are an important part of the reinterpretation's justification as being the appropriate mode in which to attack and resolve the specific scientific problems that originated the reinterpretive program in the first place.

(3) But there are serious difficulties in making the epistemologically structured arguments clear and precise. Some of these difficulties, notorious from the philosophical cases, can be given a quasi-resolution in the scientific cases, a resolution that is dependent on specific contextual aspects of the scientific problem being attacked.

(4) A number of common themes can be discerned that show important family resemblances between the nature and jus-

tification of reinterpretive strategies as they are applied in quite a wide variety of scientific cases, themes that are, at first glance, sometimes quite different from one another in important respects. These common elements in the reinterpretive program reside at a level more specific than corresponding elements in common to any imaginable epistemically motivated reinterpretive program, but more general than that of the individual, specific case.

(5) The fact that very general epistemic (and semantic) considerations function in specific scientific decisions concerning theory constructions and justifications casts doubt upon some versions of "naturalism" or "quietism" with regard to science that try to tell us that scientific theories are perfectly understandable on their own and never in need of philosophical interpretation or critique.

(6) Finally, an exploration of some of the ways in which these reinterpretive programs function within science may throw some light on how we are to view the familiar global eliminativist programs. That is, we may be able to understand global programs better as "ideal limits" of the contextually dependent scientific programs, rather than as free-standing programs for the once-and-for-all reconstruction of physical science.

What are some noteworthy cases of either the reconstruction of a theory by reinterpretation, or the replacement of one theory by another involving reinterpretation, where an ontologically eliminative process based on philosophical critique of the kind we have been discussing is invoked?

A number of such cases can be found in theories of space and time or in the theory of their contemporary unifying replacement, spacetime. Critical reconstructions of Newtonian theory reject Newton's absolute space as reference object for all motion, adopting a spacetime instead that has only the notion of a class of equally fundamental inertial reference frames, no one of which takes the place of the eliminated Newtonian base frame. In the transition from prerelativistic spacetime to the spacetime of the special theory of relativity there is an elimination, based on critique, of the notion of absolute simultaneity for events at a spatial distance from one another. The prerelativistic notion is replaced by the weaker notion of simultaneity relativized to inertial reference frames. In the replacement of Newtonian theory of gravitational force in a flat spacetime by the general relativistic curved spacetime theory of gravitation, there is a rejection of the notion of global inertial reference frames in favor of local free-fall frames or the notion of a timelike geodesic. Here again the rejection of the older theory consists in part of an ontological elimination based on a critical argument.

Such uses in physics of critical explorations suggesting ontological elimination can also be found outside the context of spacetime theories. Critical arguments for ontological elimination can be found in many places in the history of quantum mechanics: in Heisenberg's original positivistic program, in the background of Schrödinger's demonstration of the equivalence of his version of quantum mechanics with that of Heisenberg, and, very dramatically, in Bohr's Copenhagen interpretation of the theory with all its instrumentalist aspects.

More recently, arguments that invoke the critical, eliminative stance can be found in some recent discussions of the role of potentials in classical physics and in the discussion of the way in which potentials take on a radically different aspect in the quantum context, where they result in observable phenomena classically quite unexpected, such as the Bohm-Aharanov effect. This critical exploration becomes important when the search begins for a quantized version of general relativistic gravitation.

Critical eliminative arguments can be found as well in recent work on quantum field theory. For two quite distinct reasons, programs exist that propose the reconstruction of the standard theory by the elimination of its notion of "particles." Here particles are, of course, already quite different things from what they are in classical physics. In quantum field theory particles are, or are associated with, globally defined plane-waves that represent objects with definite momenta. One such critical program within quantum field theory pursues ontological elimination to avoid a deep mathematical difficulty in the formal versions of quantum field theory known as Haag's Theorem. A second such critical program, one that ends up suggesting a reconstruction similar to the first, comes about from attempting to fit quantum field theories into the curved spacetimes of general relativity.

We cannot follow up closely any of these programs here, of course, but we will be returning to them in at least a little more detail, as they serve as examples for the methodological points to be discussed.

2. FEATURES OTHER THAN CRITIQUE THAT MOTIVATE ELIMINATIVE REINTERPRETATIONS

In every case of ontological elimination founded in part upon the kind of critical arguments familiar from philosophy, there are always some specific additional scientific motives, going beyond the critical analysis itself, that drive the eliminativist program. What are some of those motives?

(A) There is the desire to formulate a new theory that will be able to deal with novel and unexpected experimental data that existing theory cannot well handle. At the same time there is a desire to deal with the new data in ways that will not introduce undesirable complexity or arbitrariness into the theory.

A prime example of this is the positing of the special theory of relativity. The original arguments for the theory are grounded by Einstein on an epistemically motivated eliminativist critique of an absolute notion of distant simultaneity. The desired end of the new theory is simultaneously to do justice to the unexpected null results of the Michelson-Morley experiments, and at the same time to avoid the arbitrariness of the Lorentz theory for dealing with those results, an approach that introduced, in Einstein's view, a groundless and arbitrary choice of one particular inertial frame as the unique aether frame in which the velocity of light was the same in all directions and had its theoretically predicted value.

(B) There is the desire to find a new theory that will do justice to old and familiar observational data, but that will do so in a manner that will be compatible with a newly established background theory, as the older theories dealing with the phenomena were not. At the same time there is a desire that the new theory eschew a kind of arbitrariness discovered to be latent in the older theory of the phenomena.

Here again the prime example is given us by Einstein. The general theory of relativity is proposed as a theory of gravitation that is compatible with special relativity in a way that the Newtonian theory is not. At the same time the new theory, by eliminating the need for global inertial reference frames by means of a critical eliminativist argument, deals with a kind of underdetermination problem latent in Newton's gravitational theory, a problem whose existence was only occasionally and vaguely sensed prior to Einstein's work. This was the inability of the older theory to determine the true inertial frames given the possibility of globally uniform gravitational fields.

(C) There is the desire to retroactively reformulate older, now discarded theories by applying to them critical eliminativist lessons learned in formulating the newer theories that replaced the older accounts.

Using many of the notions invoked in constructing the Minkowski spacetime appropriate to the special theory of relativity, one can go back and find a spacetime for Newtonian dynamics, Galilean or neo-Newtonian spacetime, that retains absolute time and the inertial reference frames of Newton's spacetime, but that disavows his reference frame for absolute velocity. The new construction is based on critical eliminativist techniques, and it reduces the underdetermination problem from which Newton's spacetime suffered, the problem of identifying which inertial reference frame constitutes absolute rest.

Similarly one can use the curved spacetime devices of general relativity to suggest a way of constructing, again in a critical eliminativist manner, a curved spacetime version of Newtonian gravitational theory that, once again, eliminates, in a prerelativistic context, the latent arbitrariness and underdetermination of the older theory. Here the advantage of the newer theory over the older is exactly that possessed by general relativity. The newer theory eliminates the underdetermination problem latent in the older theory, since in the Newtonian theory of gravity, once more, universal uniform gravitational fields were empirically inconsequential.

(D) There is the desire to reformulate a theory in order to remove from it mathematical artifacts that lead to conceptual and mathematical difficulties but that are, allegedly, neither inherent in nor necessary to the real content of the theory.

An example comes from quantum field theory, where the construction of the local algebraic approach to the theory, again involving critical eliminativist elements, is, in part, motivated by the desire to get around a mathematical consequence, Haag's Theorem, that followed from the original axiomatic formulations of the theory, and that seemed to deny the possibility of any interactions describable by the theory.

It is interesting that the same reconstruction of quantum field theory has been proposed out of motives discussed in (B) above. The move away from standard quantum field theory, with its ontology of particles, to the local algebraic theory that restricts its ontology of locally determinable measurement results, provides us with a slimmed-down version of the theory very appropriate for the task of reconciliation with a background account of spacetime as curved. This new theory fits quantum field theory into classical, prequantum, general relativity in a way not easily open to the theory in its original form.

(E) There is the desire to clarify the role of concepts in a theory, where the demand for clarification arises out of the changing roles played by these concepts as the assumed background theory changes.

As an example, consider the problem of understanding what "potentials" are in field theories. Classically thought of as just mathematical devices for computing forces, in the quantum context potentials account for a wider range of observable phenomena than can forces. These new phenomena are phase shifts that can arise in situations where the potential is not topologically simply connected. Here the program of reinterpretation is not a simple eliminativist one. However, in the scientific program of understanding the physical role potentials play in the theory, the kind of thinking that is crucially invoked is the kind involved in critical eliminativist arguments: that is, the kind of thinking that asks us what the real observational consequences of the theory are and asks how the posited theoretical features of the world contribute to these observational consequences.

Arguments of this kind play a vital role in understanding general relativity as well. For in this theory, aspects of the geometry of spacetime play the role of potentials and forces. Understanding these aspects of the theory from the critical perspective is crucial to understanding the theory philosophically, and such understanding plays a significant role both in the history of the framing of general relativity and in present projects directed toward finding formulations of general relativity suitable for constructing a quantum version of that theory.

(F) There is the desire to explain away the existence of apparently quite different physical theories that seem to be equally successful in their ability to predict the correct experimental results over a wide range of phenomena.

As an example of this, there is the program of demonstrating the equivalence of the Heisenberg and Schrödinger presentations of quantum mechanics. This program combines a critical exploration of the observational contents of the theories with the demonstration of an appropriate mathematical isomorphism at their nonobservational levels. Showing that the differences between the theories at the nonobservational level lead to identical predictions for possible outcomes of measurements and for the probabilities of these outcomes leads to the claim that the two theories amount merely to alternative "representations" of one and the same account of the world.

(G) Finally, there is the desire to offer a grand metaphysical solution to understanding the meaning of a theory that has been presented as a clear mathematical formalism but whose physical meaning is deeply problematic and even apparently contradictory.

The prime example of this is Bohr's program of embedding the measurement process as a fundamental and ineliminable structure into his interpretation of quantum mechanics, and his critical ontological-eliminativist program of taking the classically describable outcomes of measurements as the ontology of the theory. Bohr's interpretation of quantum mechanics includes an instrumentalist reading of any apparent reference to reality by the theory "between measurements." This new reading of the theory, along with the notion of the complementarity of measurement processes, is used to evade the apparent dilemmas presented by the theory in its superficially contradictory description of the world, since it seems to say that the world is simultaneously wavelike and particle-like in nature.

In every one of the cases where some version or another of ontological elimination by critical argument plays a role, then, some profound additional scientific motivation is present. Critical ontological elimination within science is not merely arbitrarily applied general empiricist philosophy.

3. COMMON ELEMENTS IN CRITICAL RECONSTRUCTIONS

I have just been emphasizing the wide variety of quite distinct motivations that can lead to an ontologically eliminative reformulation of a theory within a particular scientific context. Here I want to emphasize, in contrast, some of the elements that all of these reconstructions of theories have in common.

In each case of a reconstruction there is a claim to the effect that some difficulties with a current theory might be overcome by a procedure that eliminates from the theory one or more otiose elements of the world postulated by it. But what constitutes being otiose? A common feature of all of these scientific programs is a claim to the effect that the theory before its reconstruction possessed a richer structure than was necessary to account for all the observational phenomena. When it is claimed here that the reconstructed theory can "account for" all the same phenomena as the unreconstructed theory, what is meant is not just that the reconstructed theory can deductively generate the same observational consequences as the original theory, but that it provides just as full an explanatory account of them. Contrast this with the familiar philosophical objection to general positivism, that its empiricist reductions of theories are devoid of explanations for the observable phenomena.

The general theme of all of these cases is the theme of underdetermination. That is, the claim is that each of the unreconstructed theories allowed for the existence of many distinct possible worlds fitting its constraints where, in reality and according to the reconstructed theory, there is only one possible world. The trouble with the older theory is a familiar one: it allows for worlds that are, in principle, empirically indistinguishable from one another.

In Newtonian spacetime there are too many possible choices for the rest frame from among the inertial frames. In Lorentz theory there were too many choices allowed for an aether frame. In the theory of gravity as force in flat spacetime there are too many possible choices for the global inertial frames, both in the prerelativistic and relativistic cases. Similarly, but technically harder to explain, in the quantum-field-theoretic case there are too many unitarily nonequivalent but observationally equivalent representations available in the standard axiomatic field theory. In each case, in the unreconstructed theory's own terms, we are deprived of the possibility of using empirical experience to make the choices that theory itself claims are real choices to be made. In each case the suggestion being made is that one or more conceptual and/or empirical problem can be dealt with by, in part, an ontologically eliminativist program that replaces the older theoretical structure with one that is explanatorily its equal but that eliminates from its structure a portion of the posited world. This discardable part of the older theory's ontology is, on the older theory's own account, epistemically inaccessible to us, and is, in the light of the reconstruction, explanatorily irrelevant.

But making these claims depends upon the assumption that we are correct in believing that the entire corpus of the observational consequences of the older theory can, indeed, be saved by the reconstructed account. Without such an assumption it would not be reasonable to carry out the reconstructive program as it actually is done. There may be a role played in the theoretical change by novel observational or experimental data, like the role played by the null results of the Michelson-Morley experiment in the development of special relativity. But the actual critical reconstruction relies not on the data of experience but only on a formal investigation into the structure of the older theory, which reveals how an alternative to it, but with fewer otiose elements, can be created. However, making such an ontologically reductive move requires that we have in mind from the beginning of the procedure some idea of what is to count as the observational content of the theory, or, rather more importantly, some idea of what we can definitively count as *not* observational. Only with this a priori assurance can we legitimately claim that the reconstructed theory will indeed be able to perform the full explanatory work of its predecessor.

How are the reconstructions carried out? A full taxonomy of the possible modes of reconstruction would be very helpful but would be very difficult to formulate. But here are at least three ways in which reconstructions proceed, accompanied by relevant examples.

(1) One can collapse a multi-component structure of the original theory into a structure with only one element in the reconstructed account. This eliminates the "trade-offs" possible in the original account that led to its superfluity of possible worlds. For example, in the curved spacetime accounts of gravity, gravitational force and the structure of the global inertial reference frames are replaced by the single structure of the timelike geodesics of free-fall paths, including such paths in the presence of gravitating objects.

(2) One can find the classes of original accounts that are

observationally equivalent to one another in the older account, and identify these equivalence classes by invariants that remain the same under the transformations that take one from one member of the equivalence class to another member of the same class. One can then formulate the revised theory solely in terms of these invariants. Instead of formulating a theory in terms of potentials, for example, one can, classically, formulate it in terms of forces, where all so-called gauge-equivalent potentials generate the same forces. Quantum-mechanically, one can reformulate the theory in terms of what are called holonomies that represent the empirically relevant common content of gauge equivalent potentials in the quantum context.

(3) Alternatively one can keep the original version of the theory, but add to it an interpretive recipe for "dividing out" by its arbitrary aspects when generating empirical results. One then takes what previously counted as accounts of alternative worlds as, instead, alternative accounts of one world. Let us, once again, use potentials as an example. When one does statistical mechanics for theories invoking potentials, or when one does quantum mechanics for them using path-integral methods, one is instructed that when counting possible states of the world one is to divide the total number of states of potentials by a factor that reduces the number of states in such a way that all states represented by distinct but gauge-equivalent potentials are counted but once.

4. SOME VARIETIES OF THE NOTION OF "OBSERVATIONAL CONTENT" AND OF THE ELIMINATION OF THE UNOBSERVABLE

There is, then, a pervasive need within foundational physics to extract from a theory its observational consequences and delimit which parts of the theory outrun any legitimate role in deriving the theory's empirical consequences. Such a process of separating out the theory into its empirically necessary and empirically unnecessary components is preliminary to any program for reforming the theory by eliminating from it some parts that have caused one sort of trouble or another, and that are eliminable without loss to the genuine empirical content of the theory. Or, if one chooses not actually to eliminate the troublesome elements, one still needs the preliminary work done in order to manage those parts of the theoretical apparatus in an acceptable way when they are left in the theoretical account.

But what does it mean to talk about the "observational content" of a theory? Here the issues surrounding the relationship between the contextually relative and scientifically determined uses of that notion, and the uses of it in a prioristic and philosophical contexts, are important, subtle, and complex.

In the history of philosophy, in the context of such doctrines as phenomenalism, instrumentalism, and operationalism, there have been many attempts to capture the notion of the observational content of a theory. Some programs resort to the idea of the observable as the immediate data of perceptual awareness or the phenomenal content of consciousness. Here one faces the problems of trying to make sense of what these phenomenal contents are, and of trying to find a place for them in a naturalistic world picture. Then one has the task of trying to explain how an intersubjective, much less objective, natural science could be constructed with such subjective elements as its foundation.

Wary of mentalism and the subjectivity of sense-data, others have tried to understand the "observable" in some more physicalistic way. Facts about certain physical properties of intermediate-sized objects are taken to constitute the observable. Here the seeming arbitrariness of the selection of some physical facts as observables, and the familiar slippery-slope arguments that make any physical fact seem as observable as any other, leads to much skepticism that any useful notion of the totality of observational consequences of a theory can be formulated at all. Another attack on the problem, allegedly "naturalistic," is Quine's proposal to take such things as "causal impingements on retinas" as playing whatever useful role there would be for the notion of an observable in a regimented science.

When we look in context at the cases of ontological elimination within science, what we find, not surprisingly, is that the notion of the "observable consequences of the theory" is one that varies from case to case. The notion of observability is dependent upon the particular theory undergoing a reformulation via epistemic critique, and it is dependent upon the particular reformulation proposed and the particular critique in play.

In these critical reformulations of theories internal to science we do not find direct reference to any of the traditional empiricist/ phenomenalist notions of the "immediately present to awareness" or the "direct content of perception." Nor do issues of any alleged greater "certainty" of assertions about the observables or any alleged "knowability without any inference whatever" attributable to such assertions play any direct role in the promotion of one class or another of facts as the observable facts in the scientific cases. Nor are such notions as the physical processes governing the responses of our perceptual organs relevant in the cases from physics.

How, then, does the separation of the observable from the nonobservable proceed in the contextual scientific cases? And how is this delimitation of the one class from the other in those cases related to the traditional philosophical notions of once-and-for-all distinguishable classes of observable phenomena?

A number of the examples of theories subject to reconstruction based on critical ontological elimination were theories of space and time. Such were the theoretical reconstructions leading to the special and general theories of relativity, and those retroactive reconstructions that led to flat and curved Galilean spacetime.

Two general features characterize what is typically taken as the domain of the observable in the reformulations of spacetime theories. First, the observable is restricted to what occurs at a point, that is to say, to coincidences in spacetime. Second, the observable is taken to be restricted to relations embodied in material objects such as particles that collide or light rays that intersect one another.

The first constraint disallows our counting any feature depending upon global aspects of spacetime as being among the observable aspects of the world. In Einstein's famous original papers on special relativity it is taken for granted that coincidence among events, events such as clock readings, is legitimately considered observable, but that, for example, simultaneity among distant material events is not. In the formulation of general relativity it is such coincidences as the intersection of particle paths or of light rays, or the coincident readings of clocks, that are presupposed as exhausting the observable. Global features of spacetime, or even global features of the test particles and light rays, are excluded from the domain of the observable. A prime example of this way of thinking can be found in Einstein's realization that the kind of underdetermination, and nondeterminism, implied by the "hole argument" in general relativity presented no problem so long as one took the observational content of the theory as its real content and took that observational content to be restricted to the local coincidences among the test objects.

The second constraint forbids our counting any alleged feature of the spacetime itself as among the observables. Suppose someone tried to defend the account of gravity as flat spacetime plus forces. When confronted with the problem of the underdetermination allegedly built into it, suppose the proponent of the theory responded that the "real" global inertial frames could be determined in that account of the world simply by using direct observation, and without using material test objects. Such a theorist would just not be taken seriously by the scientific community. It is only relations among the test objects, the material particles and light rays, the measuring tapes and the clocks, that count, in the scientific context, as possible facts in the domain of the observable.

It is interesting that in the scientific discussions of the construction of spacetime theories it is sometimes alleged that restricting the observables to local relations among material objects is not sufficient. Other restrictions are sometimes thought necessary, or at least desirable, as well. There has been, for example, a longstanding discussion about which local relations among which material things provide the "best" set of observables for general relativity. In particular, there is a program designed to eliminate as observables such material measuring devices as measuring tapes, with their coincident marks, and clocks, with their coincident "ticks," and to replace them with paths of point particles and light rays and their coincidences, that is to say their intersections, as the proper observational basis for general relativity.

When we inquire into the motivation behind this program, we discover that more than one aim can play a role in the contextual choice of a class of observables. The restriction of the observables to the local and the material rests, I believe, on a kind of retreat to the more epistemically immediate that fits into a general empiricist program. The desire to eschew tapes and clocks in favor of particle and light paths has, however, a very different motivation indeed. This latter choice is based upon Einstein's injunction that a theory should be "complete," that is, that the theory should in itself offer a full explanatory account of the behavior of those elements taken as characterizing its measurement basis.

It is often claimed that explaining the behavior of material measuring tapes or clocks requires the invocation of the full theory of matter, hence of quantum mechanics, whereas it is general relativity itself that accounts for the paths of ideal free particles and light rays. In general relativity these paths are simply the timelike and null geodesics of the spacetime. There are a number of quite complex and controversial issues here, but they are not our concern. All that we need to take notice of is that the choice of what is to count as observational basis for a theory in some contextually determined scientific discussion can be motivated in multiple ways. Only some of these motivations are grounded on a general epistemically critical program.

The retreat to local features, in particular to point events characterizing coincidences, as the legitimate observables, and hence as those facts predicted by a theory that must be retained invariantly under any epistemically motivated program of ontological elimination, can be found as well outside of the reformulations of spacetime theories. If one explores the critical theorizing about potentials or gauge fields and their legitimate role in theory one finds, ultimately, a retreat to the local here also. In this case the eliminativist program is multi-staged. In the classical case it is alleged that it is the forces, not the gauge-transformable potentials, that constitute the real physical elements of the theory. In the quantum context it becomes clear in the case of potentials with a nontrivial topology, as in the example of a potential generated by a solenoid that constitutes a "hole" in its two-dimensional structure perpendicular to the solenoid, that the role of the potential goes beyond that of determining the structure of forces derivable from it. The potential also determines phase shifts of wave functions around closed loops, phase shifts that reveal themselves experimentally in interference experiments. So now these phase shifts, so-called holonomies, generated by the potential must be taken as physically real elements as well.

Further reflection would show, I think, that the elimination of potentials in favor of forces and phase shifts is itself only an intermediate step. Lurking in the background is an implicit further assumption that it is only the observational coincidences predictable on the basis of the forces and phase shifts that themselves will count, in the end, as the real physics of the situation. This can again be seen, for example, in the discussion of general relativity as a gauge theory and the response of Einstein to the "hole" argument's claim that the theory is indeterministic. I will return to the idea of some critical eliminativist program being only an intermediate stage of a larger process shortly.

Locality as a fundamental characteristic of the observable is also a theme in the critical reformulations of quantum field theory. But in this case the role played by locality is a subtle and complex one, one that is deeply interconnected to other considerations endemic to the general interpretation of the role of measurement in quantum mechanics, and one that is hard to characterize in any brief fashion.

As I noted, there are two quite distinct problems with the older versions of axiomatic quantum field theory that, curiously, can be dealt with simultaneously by a single reformulationist program. The first of these problems arises in scattering theory. One would like to think of a bunch of initially "free" particles interacting. The result of the interaction is, ultimately, some other set of noninteracting, free, particles. But it proved difficult to find a mathematical structure that would allow for a unified description of the process over the entire time of the scattering. From the axioms of the theory one can prove that there is a unique lowest energy state, a vacuum state, for the system. But distinct vacuum states are required for the asymptotic free particles and for the particles under interaction. The result of this was a theorem due to Haag that seemed to show the theory incapable of describing interactions. The difficulties here are connected with some fundamental mathematical difficulties in quantum field theory. In the quantum mechanics of systems with a finite number of degrees of freedom one can show that any representation of the quantum commutation relations is empirically equivalent to any other (the representations are transformable into one another by a unitary transformation). In quantum field theory this is no longer true and the choice of the "right" vacuum state becomes crucial.

The second problem has to do with formulating quantum field theory in a manner that would allow it to be embedded in a curved spacetime. The problems that arise here are anticipated in flat spacetimes when the world is looked at from the point of view of an accelerated observer. To that observer it is "as if" there were particles in the world that are not seen by any inertial observer. In a flat spacetime one can take the inertial observers as privileged and their particle counts as definitive. In a curved spacetime, however, there are no such privileged observers. For this reason the standard quantum field theory, a theory that assumes a definite number of particles of any kind existing in the world, becomes problematic.

One can try to resolve both of these problems in a variety of ways. The approach I want to touch on here is the local algebraic reformulation of the theory. Here the fundamental ontology of the theory is taken to be not particles, but, instead, detections of particles by spatially restricted detection devices. The theory to be constructed is one that is intended to adequately represent all possible probabilistic correlations to be found in the world between the results shown on one such body of detectors and the results determined by another collection of detectors. There is a kind of instrumentalism built into this reformulation of the theory that clearly descends from, but is differently motivated than, Bohr's invocation of measurement as fundamental and Bohr's instrumentalistic interpretation of quantum mechanics in general. The very idea of taking "detections" as fundamental in ontology is, of course, deeply problematic. But it is the other thread to this interpretation that is of interest here, the built-in assumption that all observation is, in some sense, local observation.

Obviously, the meaning of "local" here is much more problematic than it is in the spacetime cases looked at earlier. It is most assuredly not the sense of "local" that took point coincidences as fundamental. In the present reformulation of the theory one thinks of detectors as responding to particle presence in some regional open set of the spacetime. The basic idea of the earlier theory was to think of scattering as beginning with a finite number of particles sufficiently far apart that one can think of them as free, that is, as not interacting. Then the particles get close to one another and interact. Finally, after a sufficient time there is again a group of free particles. But in the newly constructed theory the positing of such free particles is thought of as representing only the probabilities of correlations between appropriate particle detections. Now there is no longer any attempt to represent the processes intermediate between initial and final detections in terms of some quantum fields whose past and future limits in time are the fields corresponding to free particles. It was that representation of things that led to the mathematical difficulties in the first place. Instead there is an instrumentalistic retreat to the earlier and later detections, which are represented mathematically by "nets" of operators over restricted spacetime regions. It is in the probabilistic correlations represented by the relations among these nets of operators that the predictive power of the theory is located.

In its other motivation, trying to do justice to quantum fields embedded in curved spacetimes, the aim of the local algebraic approach is to avoid the notion of a particle altogether. In quantum field theory, curiously, particles turn out to be global notions, since they are associated with wave fields that exist everywhere. The plane waves corresponding to the free particles of the flat spacetime theory cannot even exist in a general curved spacetime. The aim of the reconstructed theory is also to avoid the need for positing any determinate particle number, since different observers declare the numbers of particles to be different and all observers are to be treated as equally good observers. In the case of flat spacetime an accelerated observer's instruments respond "as if" there was a flux of particles in the observer's environment not noticed by inertial observers. These could be called "fictitious" particles if one liked, taking the inertial observer's count as preferred. But in curved spacetimes a similar variation in observed particle number occurs even between observers who are locally inertial, that is, are traveling timelike geodesics. Now it becomes unreasonable to credit as the "real" number of particles any one observer's detected number, except possibly in special cases where the spacetime has a symmetry that picks out some reference frames as preferred.

The local algebraic approach avoids these problems by taking particle detection in some delimited region as the basic reality posited by the theory. So here again we have a kind of localism invoked in the reconstruction. Once again it is motivated by con- textually specific problems with an existing theory. But, once again, the reformulation is rationalized in part by appeal to an epistemic critique that asks what there was posited by the original theory that we could really observe, and that reformulates that older theory by eliminating some of its traditional structure as an unnecessary and, indeed, harmful artifact.

I have been suggesting that one general theme that recurs in many ontologically eliminative reformulations of theories has been some kind of "retreat to the local." But what the local amounts to varies quite radically from case to case. In the spacetime cases there is a general invocation of material coincidences at a point as the gen- uine elements of reality that are to be preserved under any legitimate reformulation of the theory. But, as I have just noted, in the re- formulations of quantum field theory it is detections within regions, and not "at points," that are to be counted as real.

In fact there were a number of earlier critical examinations of quantum field theory, dating back to its first origins in the 1930s, that emphasized the need to *avoid* elements in the theory that referred to what happened "at a point." It was argued that formu- lating the theory in a way that was both mathematically and phys- ically satisfactory required "softening" point quantities into "spread" quantities before the observational meaning of the theory could be understood. Initially observables were thought of as represented by operators that were defined as point-valued quantities. Later the formal versions of the theory dealt with the physical observables in terms of operators that were smeared by test functions whose support (that is, whose nonzero values) is over a region. It was these region-valued, and not point-valued, quantities that were taken as the mathematical representatives of the predictive elements of the theory, that is, of the usual quantum probabilities of outcomes in the face of measurements. This move away from, rather than toward, point-like elements in the theory is one whose discussion would fall into the context of the next chapter, that is, into a discussion of how to deal with theories we regard as descriptive only of idealized aspects of the world.

A full discussion of the reconstruction of gauge theory in the quantum-mechanical context, and certainly of the reconstruction of the problem of scattering in quantum field theory or the problem of embedding that theory in a curved spacetime, could only take place against a wider background discussion of the general issues of observability and measurement in quantum-mechanical theories. This is something that we cannot pursue here. But it is important to note that no other problem in the foundations of physics has emphasized as clearly the crucial role played in the reformulation of theories by ontological elimination founded on epistemic considerations as has the measurement problem at the heart of the interpretation of quantum mechanics.

Some treatments of the measurement problem, Bohr's in particular, are largely founded on a proposed "retreat to the observable." In the case of the measurement problem in quantum mechanics, however, the notion of what is to count as "the observable" is far more problematic than it is in the cases we have been looking at. For all its problematic aspects, we do have a pretty clear grasp on the notion of the local as opposed to global quantities dealt with by a theory. And we can gain a quite precise understanding of what it is to take only the local predictions of the theory as truly dealing with elements of physical reality. But in the case of the measurement problem in quantum mechanics many of the most notorious interpretive problems arise when we try to say just what the "observable" amounts to.

These problems go back to Bohr's famous claim that there were measurement outcomes characterizable only in pre-quantum classical physical terms, a claim made despite the simultaneous claims that the quantum description of the world was itself universal in scope. Almost every position one can imagine, ranging from the claim of the universal applicability of the classical concepts (Bohmian hidden-variable realism), to versions of idealism or dualism (in Wigner's account of measurement as interaction of transcendent mind with physical world), to varieties of instrumentalism (as in Bohr's Copenhagen account), has been proposed as the appropriate framework in which to understand the role of measurement and its definitive outcomes in a quantum world in which these outcomes can be "superposed."

Again, we simply cannot explore the measurement problem in quantum mechanics here. But I do want to emphasize that, once again, in some important attempts at resolving the measurement problem we find some version of the practice of using epistemic critique to differentiate the observable elements of the theory from the unobservable, and then asking for a reformulation of the theory that preserves its predictive force among the observables without preserving the alleged problematic structure that was proposed for the unobservables. The epistemic critique is here seen playing its role within a specific theoretical problematic in foundational physics as part of an attempt at formulating the questionable physical theory in a more sensible manner.

5. DOUBTS CONCERNING NATURALISMS

Naturalism has meant very many different things to very many people, and I am not concerned in any way with trying to disentangle all of its meanings, much less with dealing with all sorts of naturalisms. One strand of naturalism, though, has been to claim that there is no point to critically engaging scientific theories from some "philosophical" point of view. On this suggestion, the scientific theories are complete and sufficient unto themselves, and they reveal to us on their face all we need to know about their "meaning" or their "interpretation." From this perspective, the perennial philosophical desire for an analysis of a theory's meaning, and the desire to reformulate or reconstruct the theory based upon considerations arising out of philosophical critique, are the pointless pursuits of will-o'-the-wisps.

But, as we have seen, there is something misguided about the suggestion that one can deal with the fundamental theories of physics in a manner that is independent of the sort of critical arguments, based on epistemic considerations, that are so familiar from empiricist philosophy. For the very construction, justification, and reconstruction of theories within the progress of science itself is replete with just that kind of reasoning we took as paradigmatically philosophical. The idea, then, that theories can be understood without reference to typically philosophical modes of thinking, especially those based on the epistemic critique of concepts and subsequent reconstruction by ontological elimination, cannot be sustained. Over and over, as we have seen, it is part and parcel of the scientific job itself to sort out the observable consequences of a theory from its unobservable consequences; to explore the part of the theory's theoretical structure that does not refer to the observables, in order to differentiate those elements essential to the theory's job of establishing correlations among the observables, from those elements that can be viewed as otiose artifacts; and then to reconstruct the theory to avoid the positing of at least some of those artifactual elements.

This would be, though, no problem for someone who is such a "naturalist" as Quine, someone, that is, who argues that scientific reasoning is exhaustive of all the reasoning there is to be done about the world, and who denies any special place for philosophical modes of thought outside of science, but who also emphasizes all along the degree to which science is itself a discipline replete with just the sort of epistemically critical thinking traditionally thought of as philosophy done in an empiricist manner. But there is reason to think that merely locating philosophical modes of thought within the construction or reconstruction of particular scientific theories is not the end of the philosophical project.

I have been emphasizing the degree to which, in each particular case, there is a special motive for carrying out the reconstructive project that goes beyond general empiricist considerations. I have argued that these additional motivations are highly dependent on the context of the specific scientific problem being addressed. I have also emphasized the degree to which the sorting out of observable from unobservable is, again, highly context-dependent. It is also clear that in many cases a great deal of idealization is involved in selecting out the observables, such as in the retreat to point coincidences in the reconstructions of spacetime theories.

On the other hand, I have been suggesting that there are general themes to be found in exploring the reconstruction process that characterize the way such reconstructions work in a manner that runs across many different particular scientific projects. For example, I have argued that it is presupposed in a wide variety of cases that what we are to count as the observational predictions of our theories must be its predictions about only what occurs locally. Here "locally" sometimes means "at a point" and sometimes "within a restricted spacetime region."

One motif of some naturalistic programs has been to argue that insofar as any distinction can be drawn between the observables and the unobservables posited by any theory, the distinction itself is one that can only be drawn by natural science. As we noted, there is also sometimes the demand that any notion of measurement used to give an interpretive reading to a theory ought to be a notion of measurement characterizable within the theory's very own range of descriptions of the natural world. Surely there are important truths in these claims. Insofar as observers and measuring instruments are parts of the natural world described by science, their structure, their functioning, and their interactions with the systems observed and measured must be a part of the domain for which natural scientific descriptions and explanations are ultimately called for.

But the repeated reliance on such maneuvers as the retreat from the global to the local concepts of a theory as a plausible mode in which to seek for an epistemically justified reconstruction of it, seems to show that we come to the task of the critical appraisal of scientific theories with some deep presuppositions about what is to count as the epistemically accessible. And it is certainly questionable whether these presuppositions are themselves consequences of some, perhaps crude and unformalized, scientific picture of the world. Does, for example, our demand that the observable be restricted to the local come from science, or is it a presupposition founded upon some kind of intuitive assurance that it is from the first-person perspective from which all knowledge is ultimately obtained?

What we need to inquire into is the degree to which it is misleading to think of all of our understanding of the world as based on our scientific world-view. If this scientific world-view is itself constructed and reconstructed, as I have argued, on the basis of programs of ontological elimination grounded in epistemic critique, and if this epistemic critique always has elements in its formulation that have their origin in some broadly presupposed empiricist view of knowledge as originating in first-person awareness, then seeking for a naturalistic perspective on the world that is grounded solely in science and that eschews any aprioristic philosophical modes of thinking may be seeking for the impossible.

This is so even if it remains true, as I have been at pains to emphasize, that in each case in which the reconstruction by ontological elimination is encountered within science, it is contextually important specific problems with the theories in question that motivate the desire for a reconstructive program in the first place, and it is the details of the theoretical situation that themselves guide us in the crucial choices to be made if the reconstruction by elimination is to be carried out.

6. THE PLACE OF GLOBAL EMPIRICIST PROGRAMS

What, from the perspective of the ongoing program of applying epistemically grounded reconstructions that work by ontological elimination in particular, context-dependent, problem situations within science, is the place in our methodology of science of such global empiricist programs as operationalism, instrumentalism, phenomenalism, and their like? Perhaps it is best to think of these proposals for once-and-for-all reductions of scientific theories to their proper observational content not as projects that can actually be carried out, but, instead, as themselves some type of idealized "limit points" to a process that is always in progress and never capable of completion.

The global programs may be thought of as abiding reminders that, at any given stage of our fundamental theorizing, we should always keep in mind the degree to which our theoretical explanatory posits contain elements that remain forever beyond the reach of direct observational determination. The global projects serve to remind us that when tackling one of the many kinds of problematic situations faced by our theories, one strategy at our disposal is to explore the option of reconstructing the theory by a program of ontological elimination founded on epistemic critique. The suggestion is, then, not to eschew "hypothesizing" altogether, in the sense in which that word was used at the end of the seventeenth century, but to be perpetually aware of the possibility that what is wrong with our theory is the result of too much unnecessary positing of theoretical structure.

There are two general objections that are often brought against the global programs of reconstructing theories by reducing them to their legitimate empirical content. First, it is denied that one can actually delimit the notion of the "observational content" of the theory in some way that serves to ground the epistemological or semantic purposes for which the notion is usually employed in empiricist reconstructions of theories. Second, it is denied that it is possible, as is often claimed in such empiricist programs, to translate the theory into some kind of finitistic account of the world framed solely in observational terms.

But the contextualized kinds of reformulations of theory with which we have been concerned do not need to characterize any sort of "ground-floor," once-and-for-all observational basis. What they do require is the conviction that, in the given context, it is legitimate to proclaim some portion of the theoretical structure in question genuinely immune to direct observational determination. Everything not explicitly excluded from the domain of the observable in the particular context is considered legitimately observable for the purposes in question. In the spacetime contexts, for example, we do not need to worry if, in some ultimate sense, particles and light rays themselves ought to be considered as not open to direct observation.

Nor are the reformulations proposals to translate all theory into its observational content. Rather, they are proposals to the effect that a theoretical structure that rejects some portion of the full ontology of the older theory is adequate for all the empirical predictive purposes and other legitimate scientific purposes, including explanatory purposes, for which the older theory was intended. And they are claims to the effect that the newer, slimmer structure is better for scientific purposes in one or more of the aspects we noted above. The reformulated theories still remain theories in a very rich sense after the limited ontological eliminations have been carried out.

Nonetheless, these reconstructive programs, with all their specific scientific motivations, are proposals to reconstruct theories in order to bring them closer to a form adequate to capturing all the intended observational consequences of the original theory, but less infected with otiose hypothesized unobservable theoretical posits than were those original, and defective, accounts of the world. To that extent they may be reasonably thought of as playing a part on an ongoing empiricist program, even if that program has no final end. From this point of view it may be best to think of global empiricist reductivist programs as Kantian ideals, one of a number of unobtainable carrots in front of the scientific donkey that, like the desire to find ultimate explanations, keeps the creature in relative progress.

Suggested Readings

A fine summary of the philosophical discussions of the role of the theoretical within science can be found in Hempel (1965). For discussions of ontological elimination in spacetime theories see chap. IV of Sklar (1974) and chaps. III and IV of Friedman (1983) on the transition from prerelativistic to special relativistic spacetime, and chap. II of Sklar (1974) and chap. V of Friedman (1983) on the transition from the older theories of gravitation to the curved spacetime of general relativity. A discussion of Heisenberg's positivism in quantum mechanics can be found in chap. 5 of Jammer (1966). Material on the role of potentials in classical and quantum mechanics is in chap. 3 of Ryder (1985). For the reformulation of quantum mechanics without "particles" see chaps. II, III, and VII of Haag (1996). On the critical, retroactive reformulation of prerelativistic spacetimes see chaps. 2 and 3 of Earman (1989) and sect. III. D. 3 of Sklar (1974). The local algebraic approach to quantum field theory is exhaustively treated in Haag (1996). For a discussion of the equivalence of the Heisenberg and Schrödinger formulations of quantum mechanics and its consequences see chap. 6 of Jammer (1966). Bohr's metaphysics is treated in Petersen (1968).

For a contemporary general philosophical discussion of empirically equivalent theories and the problem of underdetermination see sects. 41–3 of Quine (1990). For underdetermination in the context of spacetime theories see chap. IV of Sklar (1974) and chap. VII of Friedman (1983). On ontological elimination in spacetime theories see Earman (1989), chap. III of Sklar (1974) and chap. VI of Friedman (1983). For material on the "hole" argument in general relativity see chap. 9 of Earman (1989). On potentials and gauge invariants see chap. 3 of Ryder (1985) for an introduction, and Henneaux and Teitelboim (1992) for a comprehensive discussion. On the use of holonomies in reformulating theories see chap. 3 of Ryder (1985), again for a brief introduction, and Gambini and Pullin (1996) for a comprehensive discussion of the issues. For an introduction to "dividing out by the gauge" in path-integral methods see chap. 7 of Ryder (1985).

For some philosophical critiques of the general notion of "the observable" see Maxwell (1962) and Hanson (1958). On the choice of observables for framing spacetime theories see Ehlers, Pirani and Schild (1972), Marzke and Wheeler (1964), and Sklar (1985b) For a discussion of locality in quantum field theory see chaps. I and VII of Haag (1996). For the reformulation of quantum field theory in order to place it in curved spacetimes see Wald (1994). The "smearing" of quantum fields in axiomatic quantum field theory is discussed in Streater and Wightman (1964). For Bohr on measurement in quantum mechanics see chaps. 4 and 5 of Jammer (1974).

For a discussion of philosophical naturalism see Quine (1969).

3

Idealization

At different times and in different guises, a very bold and extravagant claim has recurred in philosophy. Basically the argument is that since language is only made possible by abstracting from the world, language can, therefore, not be true to the world. Languages, it is claimed, rely on words that express concepts. But the very nature of conceptualization requires focusing on one out of the infinite number of features possessed by individuals in the world. Any description of the world framed in language is, therefore, intrinsically misleading, since, being framed in words, it requires abstraction from the infinitely rich detail of the actual individual in the world. By its very nature language must be finite, and this guarantees that it cannot do descriptive justice to the infinitely complex nature of things in the world. And, it sometimes is argued, this means that no assertion in language, framed as it is in such abstractions, can be genuinely true of the world. Grand and vague claims of this sort can be found as far back as in some of the attacks on science on the part of the romanticists.

A thesis of much more modest scope, and one more familiar to analytic philosophers, is a claim that had its roots in logical atomism. Here the issue was how to deal with generalizations in language. If, as some intuitions had it, all facts were particular facts, and there were no general facts in the world, how could there be a meaningful role in language for generalizations? For didn't assertions get their meaning by corresponding to the facts?

One answer, a thesis that later recurred in a different context, was to argue that lawlike assertions ought not to be taken as making statements at all. Hence they were not true or false in any straightforward way. Therefore there need not be any facts for them to correspond to. General assertions were, rather, on this account, rules of inference. To accept a law statement was to accept the legitimacy of inferring one particular claim from another, but was not to accept a factual claim itself. But, the thesis often went on, such inference licenses had limited domains of applicability. An inference was legitimated by a generalization only for a limited domain of assumed particulars, and, perhaps, even for these only in a limited set of background contexts.

The specification of the limits of the domains of applicability of these inference rules was, however, claimed to be not itself a part of the semantic content of the lawlike assertion. Indeed, it was often claimed by methodologists that no fully explicit specification of the domain of legitimate applicability of a lawlike rule could be found, either in the assertion of the generalization itself or anywhere else in the explicitly asserted scientific context in which the generalization played a part. Rather, such domain-specificity was part of an inexplicit "practice" on the part of scientists, and not part of the explicit asserted content of accepted scientific text.

More recently, deserved attention has been directed toward another source of skepticism about counting scientific assertions as simply expressing truths, a source that bears some relation to those just noted. This is the realization that scientific generalizations are often only applicable to the world when they are qualified by some *ceteris paribus* or "everything else being equal" clause. Such qualifiers tell us that we can expect the law to hold or be applicable to a particular case only if a number of unspecified, and, perhaps, never fully specifiable, background conditions are satisfied. Even when the appropriate background situation holds, it is often argued, the law will still only be applicable to a limited degree of accuracy. And, even then, the degree of accuracy may itself not be explicitly specified or even explicitly specifiable.

Sometimes these features of the place of laws in science are dramatically emphasized by assertions to the effect that the laws are "false," or that they "lie" in what they assert about the world. Sometimes the point is made by arguing that the laws don't, and are not intended to, describe the real world at all. Rather, it is sometimes claimed, they are only intended to describe "models," abstract constructs whose features and behavior are to be somehow associated with the real features and real behavior of the real things of an irreducibly messy and complex world. This makes the connection of law assertion to real world one that is indirect and mediated by the realm of models.

Those who espouse such an account frequently claim that the applicability of laws to the world is mediated by a relation of "similarity" between the model, truly describable by the laws, and the actual system in the world. A model, it is said, is only similar to the world in certain respects, and even that only in certain contexts. It is often emphasized that the degree of similarity of model to world, and the specification of the context in which the model is sufficiently similar to the world for the laws to have genuine predictive and explanatory value, are, once again not explicit in the theory itself. The application of lawlike theory to world, then, partakes of a kind of implicit learned scientific practice, something outside the explicit content of the theory in question.

By themselves it is difficult to see how the introduction of this notion of model and the adoption of a relation of similarity of model to world will be of much help in understanding the applicability of law to world. We still are left with all the problems we may have had initially about explaining how lawlike assertions, if literally false, can be relevant to us in our predictive and explanatory tasks. For all the problems of characterizing just what the applicability of law to world consists in, and, in particular, all the original problems generated by inexactness, contextuality, and the *ceteris paribus* clause, still remain. These problems are now simply embedded in the notion of similarity, and the unpacking of that notion remains as obscure a task as was understanding the original notion of applicability of law to world.

A recent complex and subtle view of method in fundamental physics argues that scientists work in a realistic framework in which they posit entities and properties in a "phenomenological" manner. This does not mean that they are in any way restricting themselves to the observable, but only that their treatment of all of their posits is at a nonformal and "commonsense" level. They account for the behavior of their posited world by using rough-and-ready generalizations. These generalizations are not to be identified with the formal laws of our fundamental theories. Those formal laws are taken not to be genuinely descriptive of the real stuff of the world, for the reasons we have just noted. The use of the laws, rather, is "instrumental." Scientists use the laws as necessary, always in the context of their implicit, unformulated, and unformalizable practice determined by the open rules for correct application of these now instrumentalistically understood laws.

I can make only a very few brief remarks about this account of science here. I suspect that the reason the phenomenological accounts can be viewed more easily as "true" than can the formal laws of the theory is because they have so much less content. This is an example of what I will shortly call, in several contexts, a "thinning down" of content. The less a proposition says about the world, the easier it is to make it true. I am also suspicious that the account just described is a little too cavalier about the place played by the fundamental laws. It is all very well to say that these fundamental laws are "false" or that they "lie" because of the deep problems of idealization. But one should note that it becomes quite problematic how the scientist establishes reference to the entities and properties of the world in his phenomenological account, an account which deals with highly unobservable entities and properties, without taking the laws as somehow genuinely descriptive of real things. It is hard to imagine how the scientist can meaningfully talk about quarks phenomenologically, unless the reference of the term "quark" in the informal discourse has been established in the familiar way from the role it plays in the formal fundamental laws.

Here again it will be useful to explore some of these issues by working at a level that is intermediate between the details of particular cases in foundational physics and the grand generality of a global philosophical perspective. Can we find general kinds of situations within science where issues of *ceteris paribus* clauses, or other reasons for denying the literal truth of the lawlike assertions of the theory, are playing a role? We are looking for general types of cases that may encompass a number of distinct examples from a variety of theories, but where we seek for the role played within science itself by these issues of inexactness and idealization, and not for a characterization of these notions that is universally applicable and independent of the specific context of particular theories.

1. THE NON-ISOLABILITY OF SYSTEMS

A common example used to argue for the pervasiveness of *ceteris paribus* clauses implicit in the laws of science is that of a system whose internal dynamics is governed by some set of physical laws, but which is also subject to "interference" from the outside. A typical case is that of a system of molecules evolving because of the interactions among the components of the system, but where the molecules are always subject to unavoidable interference from the outside, say by the gravitational attraction exerted upon them even from distant stars.

Now if one presents the working scientist with typical versions of such examples, and tries to argue from them to the "falsity" of the laws governing the system in question, or if one tries to argue that these laws cannot be thought of as describing the real system but only as describing some model more or less similar to it, one will often be met by a shrug of indifference. The common case of a system not being exactly correctly describable by our standard scientific account of it, because the system is subject to some degree of outside interference, is not usually taken by the working scientist to be a matter of great methodological concern. Why is that? It is because the scientist believes, rightly or wrongly, that such interferences, even if unavoidable, are in general controllable.

What does "controllable" mean? The scientist believes that current scientific theory, including the substantial background theory that runs well beyond that part of current theory directly applicable to the system in question, possesses the resources necessary to tell the scientist in some cases that the outside interference is negligible. In other cases the background theory allows the scientist to compensate for the outside interference, that is, to take it into account in a broader picture of the system and its place in the world in such a way that the effects of the interference can be "subtracted off" when trying to utilize the calculations made to describe the system that rested on the originally used, internally applicable, laws.

Admittedly this notion of controllability is one that is vague and open-ended, and one that would require a great deal more in the way of explication before it could be considered truly understood and a legitimate concept to employ in methodology. But its vagueness and open-endedness is not sufficient reason to reject it as mere arm-waving or obfuscation. The mere fact that interference with systems from the outside is ubiquitous, and sometimes, even in principle, ineliminable (as is gravitational interference, which by its very nature cannot be "screened out" from the system), would be taken by most scientists as inadequate grounds for denying the applicability of the lawlike generalizations of science to the real systems themselves, or as reason to deny to science at least the aim of finding lawlike generalizations and posits about the structure of the world that are true. It is the scientist's intuition that interference is often controllable that lies at the heart of this scientific confidence.

Nevertheless, the issue of the non-isolability of systems is a fundamental one and one that should loom large in the study of scientific methodology. Philosophers have generally focused on the issue of non-isolability as one source of the difficulties encountered if we try to take scientific lawlike assertions to be exactly and unqualifiedly applicable to the real systems in the world whose behavior we wish to describe, predict, and explain. But, I believe, the issue of non-isolability has played a much more important role in fundamental physics. In a number of important cases within foundational physics the alleged non-isolability of systems, systems that are standardly treated as if they were genuinely isolable from the rest of the world, has been used as a basis on which to ground a proposed radical change in some fundamental explanatory structure. In another direction the allegation of "sufficient isolability" has played a role that goes beyond merely ratifying the reasonableness of applying a set of laws to a system in the face of ineliminable interference despite the *ceteris paribus* clauses necessitated by the interference. Propositions asserting isolability of various sorts have played a much more fundamental role in grounding a number of explanatory schemes.

Let me first outline three cases where the allegation of non-isolability of systems has played a fundamental conceptual role. In each case it is argued that some standard or orthodox version of a theory has been fundamentally flawed. And in each case the basic error of the standard theory has been alleged to be, in part, its illegitimate assumption that certain systems could be properly conceptualized as being isolated systems.

(1) In standard versions of Newtonian mechanics we deal with the dynamics of the usual systems (tops, buckets of water, solar systems) by thinking of these systems as isolated from the remaining material systems of the universe. We treat these systems by applying the fundamental dynamical laws and invoking a range of forces. Some of these forces are those the components of the system exert on one another. In some cases we allow for non-isolability of a sort by also invoking "external" forces imposed on the system from the outside. But these external forces are taken account of in the standard model of the system whose behavior we follow out as the system evolves in accordance with the dynamical laws.

From the point of view of those inspired by Mach, however, the most fundamental principle of Newtonian theory, the existence of "natural," unforced, inertial motion and the selection by it of reference frames physically distinguished as those relative to which unforced notion is uniform, is itself the result of a hidden interaction of the systems treated by the theory with the external environment, an interaction overlooked in the standard version of the theory. For Machians it is the "fixed stars," or, better, the averaged smeared-out mass of the universe, that provides the reference frame relative to which uniform motion is absolute uniform motion. Suppose we postulate that in treating the system as isolated one has made a fundamental error and that the interaction of the so-called isolated system with its external environment, the rest of the matter of the universe, is not merely the source of a correction to our usual description of the system's behavior, but is, rather, the fundamental interaction governing the system's dynamics. Assume, indeed, that it is this interaction that characterizes the difference between inertial and non-inertial motion. If such a theory can be successfully established, one would then have, for the first time, a relationistically acceptable dynamical theory.

From the Machian perspective, then, the idealization of the systems treated in standard Newtonian theory as isolated is not merely the source of some kind of controllable error that we could put to the side by adding a *ceteris paribus* clause to our account of the systems' behavior. It is, rather, a fundamental conceptual error in the theory. It is an error that leads to a total misunderstanding of the most fundamental aspects of dynamics.

(2) Thermodynamics describes the time-asymmetric changes of systems as the systems evolve from states that show macroscopic nonuniformity of such properties as density and pressure, into states that are uniform in their macroscopic features. These last states then show no further changes. This is the approach to equilibrium of an isolated system started in nonequilibrium, a change characterized formally by the time-asymmetric increase in the system's entropy. How to account for this time-asymmetrical process is a fundamental problem in the foundations of thermodynamics. And it is a central problem of the foundations of kinetic theory and statistical mechanics, the theories that try to relate the thermodynamic facts to the constitution of the macroscopic object out of its constituent parts, and the thermodynamic changes to the dynamics of those microscopic constituents.

A number of explanatory accounts in thermodynamics and statistical mechanics take the apparent isolation of the systems in question at face value. The time-asymmetric dynamical changes may then be related, in some accounts, to an alleged fundamental time asymmetry in the dynamics of the constituents of the system. Or, in other accounts, it may be credited to the special nature of the initial condition of the system characterized, again, in terms of the system's constituents and the initial conditions of these constituents. A quite different explanatory account, however, relies upon the posit that the systems treated in standard thermodynamics and statistical mechanics as isolated are not, in fact, really isolated at all.

In this last account, a number of factors are together proposed as the explanation of the time-asymmetric changes. There must be, first of all, a transformation of the order in the system accessible to macroscopic observation into an internal order that exists only in the form of detailed correlations among the states of the constituents of the macroscopic system. Thus, a gas initially confined to the left-hand side of a box later appears uniformly distributed over the box. But the information that it was at one time confined to the left-hand side is, without further postulation, still available at the microscopic level in the detailed arrangement of the molecules of the gas. Up to this point this account and the other accounts that take the system as genuinely isolated agree with one another.

But, according to the account that invokes non-isolation of the system, the real increase in entropy of the system is not fully represented by the transformation of macroscopic to microscopic order just described. Something else is needed. This final element is the dissipation of the information contained in the detailed microscopic condition of the system into the system's surrounding environment. Only this results in real irreversibility for the system. It is at this point that the fact that the system is not truly isolated from its external environment becomes crucial. Once the system has interacted with the outside world, even if that interaction is feeble indeed, the information about its original macroscopic order, now delicately encoded into the sensitive correlations among its microscopic constituents, has flown out of the system and into the innumerable number of degrees of freedom given by the components of the external world. It is this dissipation of correlations, due to fundamental non-isolability, that is alleged to account for the genuinely irreversible behavior of the original system.

Here again we have the rejection of the standard theory in favor of an alternative explanatory account. And, once again, the claim is being made that the fundamental error of the standard account was its failure to realize the incorrectness of its treatment of the systems with which it dealt as being truly isolable from their external environment. The non-isolability of systems is not, it is being argued, something that requires minor corrections to our theory, but is something that must be taken into account if one is to get the fundamental explanatory structure of the theory correct.

(3) In orthodox quantum mechanics a sharp distinction is made between the ordinary dynamical evolution of a system and the measurement of some quantity on the system. Quite distinctive formalisms describe the cases where, on the one hand, one system simply dynamically interacts with another and the future evolution of the joint system is described by the usual dynamical equation of the theory, and, on the other hand, the case where a system is acted upon by a measuring device that can be used to determine the value of some magnitude of the system.

This is the origin of the famous "collapse of the wave packet" problem in the interpretation of quantum mechanics. There have been many attempts at explaining just what it is that distinguishes a measurement process from an ordinary dynamical interaction. Some of these accounts are quite astonishingly "metaphysical," such as those that invoke "transcendent egos" interacting with the physical world (Wigner), or those that require a newly motivated kind of global instrumentalism of a very special kind for our physical theory (Bohr), or those that invoke splittings of the world into many parallel universes when measurement takes place (Everett).

But there have also been numerous attempts to try and demonstrate that the measurement process can be understood as just one species of the general genus of ordinary physical interaction. A subset of these solutions to the measurement problem have an element in common that is central to our interest here. For they rely upon the claim that the non-isolation of the system during the measuring process is fundamental to our understanding of just what that process is. Here, as in the thermodynamic case, a claim is made to the effect that the legitimacy of an account of the measuring process as one in which collapse of the wave packet occurs depends crucially on the dissipation of information in the form of correlations, now expressed in the quantum wave function of the joint system of measured object and measuring apparatus, into the many degrees of freedom of the measuring apparatus and into the many degrees of freedom of the environment surrounding the apparatus, and from which environment the system and measuring apparatus cannot be truly isolated. The claim usually takes some form of arguing that the interference terms that distinguished the original wave function of joint system and measuring device can be thrown away in the description of the system, since the non-isolation of the system makes the observational consequences of the presence of these terms irrecoverable. The claim is made that, due to the interaction of system and measuring apparatus with the external environment, a simpler, mixture wave function can be used to describe the system and the measuring apparatus. And, the argument continues, it is this simplification of the wave function that distinguishes measurement processes from ordinary dynamical interactions.

Interestingly, interpretations that are quite distinct from one another in other aspects, such as the Bohm hidden variable interpretation of measurement and the currently popular interpretation of measurement in terms of pure quantum mechanics and decoherent histories, share the common utilization of the posit of non-isolability in their characterizations of the distinctive features of the measurement process.

No one of the accounts just described, accounts relying on the denial of the legitimacy of the idealization of some system as truly isolated from the world, is an accepted part of current physical theory. Quite the contrary. Each of these accounts suffers from profound difficulties insofar as it purports to offer a complete resolution of the theoretical problem it addresses. For our purposes that is not what matters. What does matter is that in each of these cases we see a debate going on that is internal to a specific scientific problem. In each case the issue of the legitimacy or illegitimacy of idealizing some class of physical systems as genuinely isolated from the remaining universe is a crucial component of the conceptual debate about the appropriate fundamental explanatory structure for the theory in question. Disputes such as these show that the legitimacy of the form of idealization that consists in treating not-fully-isolated systems as if they were truly isolated is of much deeper importance to the conceptual debate than are the demonstrations that the ineliminable, but often quite controllable, interference in the behavior of a system requires that laws be conditioned by an implicit *ceteris paribus* clause.

In each of these cases the evaluation of the viability of the proposed problem resolution that rests upon the denial of the isolation of the system is a deep internal problem within the sciences concerned. In each case a combination of experimental and theoretical effort is needed to decide, first, whether or not the proposed solution can do the work intended for it, but, second, whether or not the solution's posit of non-isolability, of important interference with the system from the outside, is legitimate or not. Would the inertial properties of matter vary if the gross structure of the cosmos were other than it is—say, if there were no "fixed stars" at all? Would a genuinely isolated system, if one could be found, really not show the typical thermodynamic approach to equilibrium? Does collapse of the wave function occur even if the joint system of measured object and measuring apparatus remains totally isolated from the external world (as many accounts of measurement such as the account of Ghirardi, Rimini, and Weber propose)? All of these questions remain as deep open questions in the foundations of their respective sciences.

There is another way in which the issue of isolability can play a deep theoretical role within the elucidation of a specific fundamental physical theory. One of the simplest examples of how non-isolability can spoil the rigorous truth of a scientific description of a system comes from Newtonian particle dynamics. Here the evolution of a system is governed by the forces of interaction that the particles exert upon one another and that govern the accelerations of the particles. But won't it be the case, argues the proponent of the view that scientific descriptions are inevitably false to the world, that any real system will have its constituent particles subject to the gravitational forces exerted upon them by all of the particles of the universe, no matter how distant, forces that are not taken account of in our modeling of the system in question? I have suggested that some of the scientific indifference to the philosopher's claims of the inevitable falsity of the scientific descriptions comes from the scientist's conviction that it is often the case that such interferences are controllable. We can, the scientist asserts, estimate their magnitudes and assure ourselves that their influence will be "negligible enough" in the particular case under study.

But, it is important to note, the very issue of negligibility is itself one that leads to a very rich body of theory within this specific scientific context. The degree to which one particle will influence the motion of another by means of the interparticle forces generated between them is determined not only by the nature of the particles, their mass, for example, in the case of gravity, but by the spatial relationship they bear to one another. And that, in turn, is determined by the relative motions of the particles. Hence dynamics consists of a subtle feedback system in which forces determine motions that then determine future forces.

Because of this, it becomes a deep theoretical problem to determine when, in a given situation, one can treat some interparticle interaction of the system or some interference with the system from the outside as negligible and when, on the other hand, such interference must be taken into account as a major determining factor in the system's future behavior. A primary reason for this is resonance. Even a small force, if delivered with the right kind of periodicity, can have an overwhelming effect on the system on which the force is exerted. But gaining theoretical understanding of when resonances occur and when they have a non-negligible influence on the system is a very difficult theoretical problem. It was for this reason that for centuries attempts at solving such problems as the stability of the solar system remained failures. They relied on a perturbation theory that was inadequate to deal with the subtleties of resonance phenomena.

The core of much contemporary analytical dynamics amount to looking for systematic theoretical devices for dealing with such problems. Chaos theory, which studies the way in which even simple systems can have their future behavior radically dependent on vanishingly small perturbations in the system's initial states, is part of this program. From our perspective what is important is the realization that it is not the mere fact that systems are, in principle, non-isolable that matters. Nor is it the simple observation that for this reason all systems fail to meet the idealized demand that they be treatable with exact rigor as though they were isolated. Nor is it that this means that our scientific descriptions that depend on such idealizations are, therefore, always inaccurate to some degree or other. What is important is the *theoretical* problem of resonance and the instability of motion in dynamics, and the truly important insights that are gained when the real problems of isolability and non-isolability are treated in light of these issues of dynamics. For only then do we see the issue of the idealization of isolability for the truly important scientific and methodological problem that it really is.

Before leaving this topic, it might be helpful to discuss briefly another way in which the issue of the isolability of systems plays an important role in foundational physics. Here I want to focus on some positive roles the assumption of isolability plays, roles that go far beyond the merely negative role of assuming that interference from the outside may be neglected.

In formalized quantum field theory a fundamental role is played by a posit designed to capture the idea that causal interactions between events are limited by the relativisitic principle that no causal influence can propagate faster than the speed of light in a vacuum. In every attempt to find a rigorous formulation for the theory (an ongoing and extremely difficult project, as the naive theory is replete with mathematical and conceptual problems that gravely interfere with understanding it clearly), some place is found for such a "causality principle." One standard version is the axiomatic postulation that the commutators of the operators that mathematically represent the field quantities must vanish for points in spacetime that are spacelike separated from one another, that is, that are such that no causal signal can connect them. This limitation on the possible causal influences of one event upon another, we should note, is in no way incompatible with the famous quantum-mechanical result that there are curious probabilistic correlations among the outcomes of experiments at spacelike separations that cannot be accounted for in terms of local hidden variables carrying information to them from past causal connections. This kind of imposition from relativity, that there is a fundamental limit to causal connectibility that must be built into any theory compatible with the background assumption of a relativistic spacetime, leads to a kind of presupposed guarantee of isolability unlike any such notion encountered in prerelativistic physics.

A different kind of assumption of isolability, one more closely related to the notion of isolability discussed in our earlier examples, also plays a role in some foundational accounts of quantum field theory. This is the so-called "cluster decomposition principle." In the words of Weinberg, "It is one of the fundamental principles of physics (indeed of all science) that experiments that are sufficiently separated in space have unrelated results. The probabilities for various collisions measured at Fermilab should not depend on what sort of experiments are being done at CERN." The formalization of this thought, the cluster decomposition principle, can be added to the other important assumptions of the theory. Basically the other principles include those of relativity and quantum mechanics and the assumption that the scattering of particles can be modeled by means of a so-called "S-matrix" (scattering matrix) that can be generated from the Hamiltonian function that represents the energetic interactions among the particles scattered. The cluster decomposition principle, when added to these other postulates, can go a long way in explaining why the standard theory can, all along, be framed as it is. That is, it explains why it can be framed in terms of creation and annihilation operators for the particles, combined with basic principles of the conservation of energy and momentum applied in the standard way.

Here we have an attempt to reconstruct an existing theory, quantum field theory, in a manner that is somewhat independent of its historical origins, but that is more clearly indicative of the fundamental physical principles underlying the formalism. Instead of starting with intuitive notions of fields and their decomposition into Fourier components, which in the light of quantization led to the orthodox formalism in the first place, we have a derivation of the theory from first principles that emphasizes the crucial role played by a basic posit of the isolability of experiments.

Weinberg's remark that such a principle is fundamental to "all science" is also highly suggestive and very important. The intuitive idea is that without a sufficient degree of isolability of systems we could never arrive at any lawlike regularities for describing the world at all. For unless systems were sufficiently independent of one another in their behavior, the understanding of the evolution of even the smallest part of the universe would mean keeping track of the behavior of all of its constituents. It is hard to see how the means for prediction and explanation could ever be found in such a world.

For all the truth to the claim that the standard presupposition of the isolation of a system is merely an idealization, it is arguable that the interference from the outside is often controllable, and that the idealization is therefore often legitimate. But if the claim just discussed is also correct, then it can be argued that unless such idealization of isolability were sufficiently legitimate in a sufficiently dominant domain of cases, we could not have any science at all.

2. THE PARTIAL NATURE OF THEORIES

There is another source of the need to view scientific descriptions as idealized and another ground for denying truth to scientific assertions that is related to, but distinct from, the alleged non-isolability of systems. This other source of the need to idealize lies in the fact that our theories provide only partial accounts of the world. No one theory gives us a total description of how things are. Each accounts for only its own portion of the natural world. The partial nature of theories is connected in important ways with another issue, one that I wish to postpone for the present. This other issue is the fact that any given theory is usually thought of as only the temporary theory of its domain, a theory that will in the future be replaced by a deeper theory. The later theory may be one that will integrate the contemporary partial theory into a theory that extends over a much wider domain of phenomena. At this point it is not any of the issues of the transience of theories with which I want to concern myself, but only with the partial nature of theories within the science of any fixed, given time.

A standard example to illustrate the partial nature of theories is that of a test object having its motion affected by forces that are the result of its relationships to other objects. Here, it is often emphasized, a prediction or explanation of the test object's motion that takes into account only one kind of interaction that the test object has with external particles, or with imposed fields, can never provide a truly reliable prediction or a truly adequate explanation of the test object's behavior; for the motion of the test object that is to be predicted or explained is not the result of only the one force taken into account, but the result of all the causal agencies acting on the system.

Here again it is useful to note that the concerns expressed by philosophers of science about the inadequacy of any scientific account due to that account's partial nature are concerns that are frequently brushed aside by the working scientist. The reason for this studied indifference on the part of the practitioners of science is similar to the reason that leaves so many of them indifferent when global issues of non-isolability are brought to their attention. This is the fact that in many circumstances the errors introduced by neglecting forces other than those dealt with in the theory being applied are controllable errors. Sometimes the result of these other forces can be known, on the basis of the entire background theory of the time, to be unimportant. That is, there is good scientific reason to think that, were they taken into account, the predicted motion of the test object would not vary greatly from its motion as predicted when only the one force under consideration is taken into account. In other cases the errors introduced by ignoring the other forces may be substantial, but the scientist may be working in a context where their marginal effect on the system is being taken into account in some other part of the predictive and explanatory program.

I don't deny that the general issue of controllability is a tricky one. It would be quite a task to say what, in general, controllability comes down to. One wonders if the notion can be given any fully transparent form in a way that applies over a wide range of scientific cases. It may very well be that the applicability of the notion of controllability is so context-dependent that a general notion of it could be, at best, only a loose collection of more precise notions grouped together by a sort of Wittgensteinian family resemblance.

There is a standard move that is made when the issue of the partial nature of theories is raised. Again it receives its clearest illustration in the case of a test system whose motion we wish to predict or explain. In the context of classical physics, motion is accounted for by the introduction of the theoretical intermediary of forces.

When subject to forces the test system deviates from what would otherwise be its natural, inertial, motion. But what if the test system is undergoing many different kinds of interaction with its environment? Well, we can think of each type of interaction as generating its own kind of force to which the test system is subject. So if it interacts with all matter gravitationally it is subject to gravitational force, if it is electrically charged it is subject to electrical force, and so on. Finally the change of motion the test system experiences is the cumulative change that sums up the changes induced by each type of force. We can then, as has been often pointed out, try to save the truth of our lawlike assertions by framing them in terms of such types of forces, or force components, instead of in terms of force in general. Whereas the force a particle feels will not in general obey an inverse square law, the gravitational force it suffers may very well do so.

What we see here is a process that, as we shall later note in more detail, plays a number of quite distinct roles in allowing us to save the truth of our assertions in the face of claims to their inadequacy. Here we see it at work in trying to keep the laws true despite their clearly partial nature in describing the world. The process works by reducing the content of the assertion in question. The law is taken not to be about force, but about a force kind or force component. There are other ways as well in which such reduction of content can be introduced to save truth. The most trivial of these is the one that many have noted before where we reduce the content of some claim involving magnitudes by, say, replacing in the assertion some claim about the exact value of a magnitude by a claim about a range or spread of values. Instead of claiming that $f(a) = b$, for example, we can claim that $f(a)$ is in some range of values, say between b' and b'' inclusive. Other, less trivially formalizable, moves follow the same theme. Weaken the content of an assertion that one takes to be not rigorously true but only approximately true, and one can, perhaps, replace it by another related assertion whose unexceptionable truth is obtained by a reduction in its contentful claims.

This is an instance of the process of "thinning the content" of our assertions. If, for example, an assertion cannot be taken as strictly true because it deals only partially with the world, thin out its content and one raises the odds that one will have an assertion that is true, or, at least, that is "closer to the truth." Once an assertion's content has been thinned, of course, it says less about the world. It may then become problematic how it is to be applied to the world in any specific case of a demand for prediction or explanation. If we wish to predict the future motion of a particle, our recipe for applying a law of gravitational force must be more complicated than would be a recipe for applying a law of force *simpliciter*. In Newtonian mechanics we need only identify acceleration with applied total force. But if we want to predict actual acceleration, and not just "acceleration due to gravity," we will need to apply the law of gravitational force only in the appropriate background context of a specification of the other relevant forces ignored by the more limited law.

Ought we to consider such componential entities as the gravitational force or the component of acceleration due to gravity as real entities in the world? Or should we take them to be only fictive, even if we accept full force and full acceleration as real? I doubt if there really is much of an ontological issue to be debated here. Objects can be divided up by us into spatial parts in innumerable ways. That is no reason for denying the reality of any of those parts. The same goes for dividing processes up into temporal stages or parts. There seems to be little reason for denying reality to parts of other kinds of entities, once those entities themselves are accepted into the furniture of the world, even if the notion of "part" in question is not simply spatial or temporal. We can decompose vector quantities such as forces and motions into their components by vector decomposition and we can decompose fields into their plane-wave elements by Fourier analysis. There seems little metaphysical cost in accepting such components as being as real as the entity they compose, in whatever manner of composition one has in mind.

What is important about the partial aspect of theories is the way in which such incompleteness can be handled within the background scientific context. We know, for example, that changes of motion are mediated by a variety of relations the test system has to other entities in the world, whether other objects or pure fields. And we know that if a number of such relations are simultaneously realized, all must be taken into account when the full change of motion is to be correctly described or predicted. It doesn't matter much how one views this additivity of effects, whether as the real sum of real components or as, instead, the only real thing whose components are fictive elements in a pseudo-decomposition. What matters, first of all, is that separable laws correlating change of motion to the causal situations in their pure, one-component form can be found. And what also matters is that additional principles can be discovered that tell us how these laws can be jointly applied when multiple application is called for.

More interesting than the ontological issue is the nature of the principles for multiple applicability. The most important of these principles is that of linearity. In some circumstances one can take the effect of imposing a variety of distinct forces on a test system as being some simple additive result of the effect of imposing each force separately. It is this that allows us to speak of a total force vector whose components are the forces of the various kinds, and not just the spatial components of some one kind of force. Even when linearity holds, taking account of multiple forces may not be at all simple. The net electrostatic force a charged particle feels will depend upon its separation from other charged objects. This will depend on its motion, and that will depend upon all the other forces present. But when linearity holds we will not need to adjust our estimate of the amount of electrostatic force on an object when it is in a specific position to take account of what other forces are acting on it simultaneously.

Violations of linearity are important. The most famous example is one that is, perhaps, more an issue of isolability than it is of partialness, but we might still mention it here. Our contemporary theory of gravity, general relativity, is a dramatically nonlinear theory. Crudely, gravity is the coupling of all mass-energy to all other mass-energy. But when a gravitational interaction takes place between, say, two particles, the very energy of the interaction must be taken into account when estimating the mass-energy distribution that results, and, hence, the resulting field of gravitational force. There is no hope, then, that the interaction of a test particle with two other gravitating particles, say, can be derived by simply summing the result of its interaction with each other object separately. And, as has often been clearly pointed out, there are many other cases where the result of imposing two causes simultaneously on a test system results in a change in that test object that is in no useful sense the simple sum of the effects that would result from applying each cause by itself.

There is no question, then, that those who emphasize to us the partial nature of our laws and theories are focusing our attention upon important methodological matters. Nor is it useful to challenge the claim that a fundamental consequence of this partial nature of individual theories is that no rigorously true description of the full behavior of things in the world can be given by any account that pays attention to only one of the theories at any time. I doubt, however, that it will be very helpful to deal with these issues by claiming that the individual theories are applicable only to models, where here the model is taken to be an ideal system affected only by a single causal factor. The proponent of the account that invokes models then introduces a notion of similarity of model to world to mediate the indirect applicability of the individual theories to the world of real systems multiply affected. There are, as just emphasized, real concerns about how to describe the applicability of a partial account to a world of many causes. Such concerns are located in the real questions about how multiple causes jointly determine single effects. But, to repeat an earlier argument, all of the real issues will have to be addressed in explaining what "similarity" of model to world can consist in, and these will be the same issues that would be directly confronted if we took the individual theories to be directly applicable to the real world while acknowledging the complexities inherent in the notion of applicability that arise out of the partial nature of each theory taken by itself.

Controllability is certainly a matter central to understanding the issue. It provides the optimistic assessment of the working scientific community that things can often proceed satisfactorily even if we deal with prediction and explanation on a very piecemeal basis, one partial set of laws or theories at a time. The device of thinning content can also sometimes provide a useful semantic framework for handling a group of partial accounts by dealing out to each account its own partial effects.

But the issues of greater scientific importance, and the issues which can provide us with a richer diet of methodologically interesting problems, are those that focus on just how the scientific context can itself be used to provide us with rules and principles for managing partialness and for allowing us to assimilate numerous partial accounts into more complete "total" accounts. Here the nature and limits on linearity assumptions or on more complex rules for joining multiple causes together need to be explored. An investigation into how partial causes are separated out by science, how partial laws and theories are evidentially tested in the light of the ineliminability of effects not taken account of by the partial theory under examination, and how the partial accounts are then simultaneously brought to bear, would uncover much that remains hidden. One wonders also if Weinberg's remarks are applicable here: Is the very possibility of dealing with separate causes in separate scientific investigations, like the possibility of dealing with not-really-isolated systems as though they really were isolated, a precondition for our discovering the laws in the first place?

I will have something more to say about a very special kind of partial nature of theory, and a very special method proposed to deal with that partialness of theory, in section 5 of the following chapter.

3. THE ROLE OF LIMITS

There are many cases where, in order to find an object to which some law or theory applies exactly or rigorously, one must invoke the notion of a system that is characterized as the "limiting system" of some more realistic system. This supplies us with another range of cases to support an argument to the effect that the laws and theories of science are strictly false if they are thought of as applying to real systems in the world. Laws are often true only "in the limit." A natural extension of this thought, is, as before, to declare the laws and theories true only of models constructed using the limiting process in question, and then to push the issue of the applicability of the laws and theories to the real world on to the problem of characterizing similarity of model to world.

As in the previous cases of isolability and partialness, I would argue that invoking the notions of model and similarity, while harmless and perhaps convenient, doesn't get one very far in understanding the relationships the laws and theories in question bear to the real system in the world. And, as before, I would argue that there are many cases where the fact that our laws and theories apply rigorously only to idealized limiting cases of real systems is taken by the scientific community, and rightly, as grounds only for moderate concern. Once more these are examples where the use of the idealization of taking limiting cases is highly controllable by the background science.

This controllability of the limiting idealization can take on a number of distinct forms. For example, consider motion that is affected by some kind of frictional force in addition to the applied forces under consideration. In many cases we can give an idealized account of the motion by treating the system as if the frictional forces were absent, or "in the limit of zero friction." The idealized treatment is legitimated by some part of the theory itself that tells us the degree to which the idealization will fail when the frictional forces are not exactly zero. The auxiliary account that enables us to deal with the issue of how severe our idealization has been might consist of a more general solution to the problem at hand that applies when frictional forces are taken into account. This then allows us a comparison between our idealized solutions and the solutions obtained when a less idealized description of the system is invoked.

But we need not even have such a more general solution. In some cases our theory will enable us to frame estimates of the maximal degree to which a more exact solution will differ for some range of parameters from our idealized solution. Such estimates may be calculable even when our theory is inadequate to provide us with the full details of the solution that is obtained when the idealization is dropped. An especially interesting instance of such theoretical control over idealization appears in the theory of structural stability that is a component of the general theory of dynamical systems. For many kinds of systems, structural stability theory can be used to inform us that many qualitative features of the motion we predict when we use the idealized account will be preserved when the move to a less idealized account is made. For example, structural stability theory can sometimes tell us that the structure of the attractors of motion, states of motion to which the motion of the system will evolve over long time periods of time, will remain the same as they can be calculated to be when the solutions to the idealized case are derived, as long as the deviation of the real system from the ideal remains within certain specifiable limits. In these cases, then, we can be assured that if our interest is in the qualitative global dynamical structure of the motion, and not in its quantitative local details, we can rest assured that our invocation of idealized conditions in our solution to the course of motion has not introduced error into our account. Our theory tells us that, even were we to give a more exact characterization of a less idealized system, the *structural* features of the motion would be predicted to be the same as those predicted from the idealized case.

But it is the cases where controllability does not exist that are more interesting from a methodological and philosophical perspective. Here the role played by "going to the limit" and working in that idealized context is much more subtle. In these cases, major efforts of theoretical science are sometimes required in order to understand just how the role of limits is functioning in our theoretical understanding. And deep issues of the very legitimacy of idealizing by going to the limit arise in these uncontrollable cases. For the methodologist, one issue that arises is whether one can sort out general types of such subtle theoretical moves that take the form of introducing idealizing limits of these more radical sorts.

A wide variety of such less tractable idealizations that work by going to some limit can be found in the theories that try to construct an understanding of the behavior of the macroscopic world by exploring its constitution out of vast numbers of microscopic constituents, especially in those theories that invoke probabilistic elements at the microscopic level, as in statistical mechanics. Here it is often the case that we have available to us a theory framed in terms of macroscopically accessible features of systems that obey a deeply systematic set of laws that govern the interaction of those macroscopic features, such as the laws of thermodynamics and the more specialized laws governing macroscopic objects of various types. We also have a detailed understanding of the way in which the macroscopic object is composed out of the microscopic constituents. The microscopic components are described without using the special macroscopic features that appear in the macroscopic theory. And the behavior of the microscopic components is governed by known dynamical laws and by the specific forces that describe the interactions of the microscopic components with one another. The special macroscopic laws, the thermodynamic principles, play no role in this microscopic description. The grand program is to construct a predictive and explanatory account of the behavior of the macroscopic objects that takes as its fundamental premises the constitution of these objects out of their microscopic components and the laws governing the behavior of those components.

Two such interlinked attempts at grounding the macroscopic on the microscopic are the efforts to found hydrodynamics and thermodynamics on the fundamental constitution of matter, which is taken to be the composition of macroscopic things out of a vast number of interacting molecular components. In both cases the original theories of the macroscopic are framed in terms of continuum concepts, with the macroscopic matter treated as though it were continuous with densities at every point, and as though it possessed continuous macroscopic features such as fields of velocities or of temperatures. The underlying theory of composition, however, tells us that this idealization of continuity is misleading and that the macroscopic objects are actually constructed of discrete elements.

The program of trying to fully understand the "reductive" relationship between the macroscopic theories and those characterizing the microscopic realm is one of enormous difficulty. Especially in the case of thermodynamics, it is fair to say that many deep controversies exist about how the relationship between macroscopic and microscopic accounts is to be understood. Indeed, there are many who would deny that anything appropriately called a "reductive" relationship can exist between the theories at the two levels at all. In order to ground the macroscopic theory on the microscopic account, it is necessary to introduce into the latter fundamental posits of a probabilistic nature. These appear to go beyond anything contained in the nature of the composition of the macroscopic object out of its microscopic components, and, arguably, they go beyond anything that can be derived from the dynamical laws governing the microscopic realm as well. What these probabilistic posits ought to be, how they are to function in the explanatory role allotted them, and how they are themselves to be explanatorily accounted for, all remain deep open issues in the foundations of the theory. We will be able only to touch lightly on these issues here.

What I do want to focus on are the numerous ways in which idealizations, idealizations that work by dealing with limiting cases, function in these statistical-mechanical accounts. When one explores the theory one sees repeated usage of limit-type reasoning when one tries to go from the probabilistically structured body of assertions about what happens at the microscopic level to the desired lawlike descriptions of what goes on at the macroscopic level. These uses of limiting procedures to obtain the desired results are of many quite different kinds. Some of them resemble the kinds of manageable, controllable, limit-type reasoning just discussed. But other examples of limit-type reasoning in statistical mechanics seem very different in their nature, introducing a variety of "uncontrollable" results. In addition, the role played by the use of limits in the theory often has a much deeper, and more controversial, theoretical and conceptual role than that role played by the use of limiting procedures where it is only the neglect of marginally effective residues that is being obtained by working in the limit.

One kind of limit that plays a ubiquitous role is that of dealing with a system thought of as being infinitely large in size, that is, of having infinite volume. In this limit one also thinks of the system as being constituted by an infinite number of microscopic components. But the density of the idealized system is supposed to equal that of the real, finite system under consideration. This is the so-called thermodynamic limit.

This limit plays many important roles in the theory. It is used to allow the theoretician to disregard the "edge effects" that are due to the fact that the system in question meets the outside world in the form of the walls of its container (say a gas in a box). This role is an innocuous, controllable kind of going to the limit. The thermodynamic limit is also used to justify the assumption that a number of distinct ways of introducing probabilistic considerations into the theory will give rise to equivalent results when predictions are made with them about the macroscopic behavior of the system. In the theory this is known as showing the "equivalence of ensembles [for example, micro-canonical and canonical] in the thermodynamic limit." Another very important role of the thermodynamic limit is its use to justify the assumption that average values calculated using the introduced probability assumption can be identified with most-probable values calculated using the same probability distribution. This identification of two distinct probabilistic quantities plays an important part in some rationales that account for the explanatory roles that can be legitimately played by theories that invoke the identification of average values with the observed macroscopic features of the system. And in the theory that accounts for phase transitions at the macroscopic level, the thermodynamic limit idealization is used to derive the sharp transitions of features that are posited in the (idealized) macroscopic theory and that are unobtainable in the statistical theory if one sticks to finite systems. Most fundamentally, the thermodynamic limit is also used to show that the quantities calculated at the probabilistic microscopic level that are "identified" with the macroscopic features will have the formal properties necessary for such an identification to be made, for example, that the statistical mechanical entropy will be, as desired, an extensive (additive) property of the system.

It is interesting that in a number of the applications of this limiting process controllability exists. In these cases our theory can, indeed, give us estimates as to the degree to which we can expect our real, finite systems to deviate in their behavior from the behavior predicted by the theory for the idealized, infinite volume and infinite component system. We can, for example, gain control over their magnitude of various fluctuational phenomena that will afflict finite systems but will disappear in the thermodynamic limit. This will give us estimates as to how the various ensembles will prove, for finite systems, not fully equivalent to one another. And we can, for another example, estimate the magnitudes of the edge effects that afflict finite systems.

The thermodynamic limit is, however, not the only important limit invoked by the theory. Other arguments frequently advert, for example, to temporal limits. Quite frequently results can only be obtained by asking about the kind of behavior we can expect from the system "in the limit as time goes to infinity." The use of such limits is sometimes rationalized by arguments to the effect that our macroscopic measurements take very long times compared to the typical times associated with molecular processes. But such rationalizations of the use of the limit are notoriously tendentious and are usually eschewed by careful theorists.

One typical use of a limit as time goes to infinity is in the program of showing that a probability distribution appropriate to a system of a given kind will, even if initially not a probability appropriate to the equilibrium condition of the system, evolve as time goes to infinity to a probability appropriate to equilibrium. We should note that the systems in question are already characterized by a number of questionable idealizations in their theoretical description. And we should note that the approach to equilibrium of the probability distribution is only an approach in what is called a "coarse-grained" sense. Such behavior of the probability distribution over time is called "mixing." Nevertheless, invoking such limiting behavior for the probability distribution is often part of the program of explaining why systems started in nonequilibrium move to an equilibrium condition.

This use of a limit is one that is often interestingly uncontrollable. For example, nothing in the result that tells us that, in some sense, equilibrium is obtained in the limit of infinite time gives us any grounds for inferring what will happen in any specific finite time. For all we know, the system could spend vast time periods far from equilibrium, or even spend vast time periods moving away from equilibrium rather than closer to it. But what we really would like from our theory would be predictive and explanatory accounts of the monotonic finite-time approach to equilibrium we expect to find from actual systems in the world. At this point the philosopher may be reminded of alleged justifications of induction that tell us only that induction will work "in the long run," that is, in the limit of an infinite number of observations, but give us no reason to expect success with it in the short run.

There are other, even subtler, cases of uncontrollable limits invoked in the atomic-probabilistic account of macroscopic thermodynamic behavior. One kind of limiting idealization is the Boltzmann-Grad limit. It is thought to be appropriate for studying gases of low density, since it asks what happens in the limit as the number of particles, n, goes to infinity but the size of the molecules, d, goes to zero, with nd^2 staying constant. This implies that in this limit the density of the gas goes to zero. This idealization is used in an attempt at deriving the full, finite-time, nonequilibrium behavior of a system. The aim is to derive in a rigorous manner the famous Boltzmann equation. This equation, which describes the approach to equilibrium of a dilute gas, was derived by Boltzmann (and others) only by using probabilistic posits that are hard to rationalize in the overall theory. The problem with these posits is that they must be made for each moment of time. This is of dubious consistency, since the probabilities at different times are not independent of one another. The new account uses a much less controversial probabilistic assumption, one that assumes "randomness" only at a single moment. One is able to derive the desired equation, but one is only able to show that it holds for uninterestingly short time periods. There is reason to believe that the results may hold for longer time periods, indeed for time periods of physical interest. But, curiously, there is also reason to believe that the arbitrarily long-time extension of the results will only hold for systems that meet the limiting idealization condition exactly. That is, it is very doubtful that the results can be extended to hold as "approximately true" in the arbitrarily long-time case even for systems that deviate from the ideal case by any small amount whatsoever. Hence we have, once again, the application of a limiting procedure as an idealization that shows interestingly uncontrollable aspects.

The place of this idealization in the theory is of methodological interest for other reasons as well. What, precisely, is the explanatory role in the theory of the idealization that consists in going to the limit of an infinite number of microscopic components constituting the system? From one perspective, that of ergodic theory and ensemble mixing (the usual perspective in which results are obtained in the ideal limit of time going to infinity), the place of the idealization of an infinite number of components is restricted. Its only role is to assure us that the probability distributions essential to the theory will be strongly peaked around a single value. From this perspective all the results obtained by the other idealizations remain true even in the case of finitely composed systems, even if there are only a few particles in the system. It is just that these results are less useful in such cases because the probabilities for states will be broadly spread out, rather than sharply focused on single macroscopic values as is the case when the number of components is large.

But from the perspective of the rigorous derivation of the Boltzmann equation, the role of the idealization of infinite numbers of components is far more central. Only in the Boltzmann-Grad limit can the desired results be obtained. It is far from clear what these results can tell us, if anything, about systems with small numbers of components.

It is important to note that the standard "mixing"-type rationalizations of nonequilibrium statistical mechanics are in deep conceptual conflict with the rationalization that uses the Boltzmann-Grad limit. Although there is no formal mathematical contradiction between the results obtained in the two approaches, the two idealizations seek the explanation of nonequilibrium behavior in radically distinct idealizations.

At the present time there is no agreed understanding of what the conceptual structure ought to be for the theory that combines an understanding of the composition of macroscopic objects out of their microscopic components, the theory of the dynamical interaction of those components, and a number of probabilistic posits, in order to construct an explanatory account of the lawlike behavior of the macroscopic world in its thermodynamic aspects. There are a number of reasons why strong disagreements exist in the interpretation of statistical mechanics. Some of these disagreements have to do with the nature of the basic probabilistic posits, their justifications, and their proper roles in an explanatory account. But other disputes have at their core disagreements about the proper roles to be played in the theory by one or another idealization that is constructed by invoking some limiting procedure. The nature of the appropriate limits, their suitability for realistically representing real physical systems, and their place in the explanatory structure of the theory all remain controversial.

Not surprisingly, the programs designed to resolve these disputes about the role of idealizations in the theory combine general methodological considerations, such as those dealing with the very nature of probabilistic explanation, with considerations drawn from the experimental and theoretical science itself. Just as in the case of the issues concerning the isolability of systems, though, what we discover is that most of the interesting questions about the role of idealization in the theory are not those that first occur to the philosophical methodologist. The fact that the introduction of limiting idealizations makes the nature of our theoretical models different from the precise nature of real physical systems or real physical processes does not by itself cause the scientist much concern. When the procedure of idealization by going to a limit has a transparent, controllable nature, the fact that the laws are laws only of ideal models causes no dismay. It is, rather, in those cases where the choice of appropriate limit is not fixed in any obvious way by our embedding background theory, and where the deep structural role played in our explanatory account by working in the limit is itself a matter of theoretical controversy, that the issues of idealization that truly concern the working scientist appear. And, I suggest, it is in these kinds of issues that the philosophical methodologist will find the richest vein of interesting issues as well.

We might note here that there is another role limiting processes play in foundational physics that is of deep conceptual interest. This is in relating some older theory to a newer replacement to which the older theory is thought to "approximately reduce." The relations of Newtonian mechanics and gravitational theory to special and general relativity and of Newtonian mechanics to quantum theory are said to be of this nature. In both cases, "going to a limit" plays a crucial role: in the first case, in letting the velocity of light go off to infinity, and in the second, in letting Planck's constant be "very small." Suffice it to say here that, especially in the case of the relation of classical physics to quantum mechanics, the role played by limiting processes is very subtle and complex indeed.

4. MODELS

The ubiquity of the role of models in theoretical science has been pointed out again and again by methodologists. We continually see scientists describing systems "as if" they were systems of some more familiar kind, for example. Treating the systems in this "pretend" way often provides a royal route into gaining predictive and explanatory control over the systems in question. At the same time we are often warned about the mistake of taking the real system to be truly similar to the model in all respects. We learn a lot about molecules and their interactions as components of a dilute gas when we offer an account of their dynamics that treats them as if they were hard-sphere billiard balls colliding in a box. But everyone knows that molecules are quite unlike billiard balls in many respects. They are even quite unlike billiard balls when it is simply their dynamical interactions under collisions that are our sole concern. We learn a lot about nuclear fission by treating the nucleus as if it were a water droplet characterizable by molecular cohesion resulting in surface tension. But even in the fission process itself, the nucleus behaves, in many different respects, very unlike a splitting water droplet

A serious attempt at characterizing all the varied roles that models can play in the construction, testing, and application of theories for predictive and explanatory purposes would be a vast undertaking. Models come in an enormous variety of forms and are utilized in an enormous variety of ways. Although many examples of the modeling process have been discussed in the methodological literature, and although a number of trenchant and helpful observations have been made about how they function in their various roles within science, we are far from having any carefully worked-out and exhaustive characterization of what they are like and how they function in all their manifold forms and roles. Here I intend only to make some very brief and grossly general remarks about how the notion of modeling can, and cannot, help us in our methodological pursuits.

First let me repeat my intuition that resort to the notion of a model will be of little help when the issues that concern us are the semantic connections that hold between our theories and the real world to which the theories are intended to apply. If we are disturbed by the fact that almost none of the deeply theoretical assertions that we make in foundational science can be rigorously held to be true of the systems about which they make descriptive claims, I doubt that we can gain any relief by invoking the notion of models. If we take the scientific assertions to be intended to be true only of the models, and not of the messy real-world systems themselves, we will still need to understand the ultimate relations which the assertions bear to the real-world things and their features. The suggestion that this relation can be analyzed in a twofold, indirect, manner by taking the assertions as true, *simpliciter*, of the models and then taking the models to be related to the real systems by some relation of "resemblance," gains one, as I have claimed before, little by itself. For we still are left with the problem of understanding what "resemblance" is to be taken to be. Abstractly, I suppose, that is easy enough: the model and real system will share some features but will differ in others. But exactly how the "sharing" of features is to be construed from case to case is, of course, where all the interesting philosophical analysis will lie. The basic point is that if we have the resources to understand that notion, won't just those resources serve to characterize the complex semantic relation that the assertions would have to bear to the real systems, were we to analyze the relationship of language to world directly in the first place? If that isn't so, why isn't it so? Talk of models is a useful way of characterizing many of the aspects of idealization that we have touched on earlier. But it is much less promising as an effective route to understanding the semantics of theories.

Next I want to emphasize two different roles "models" might play. First there are the cases where the scientist is quite certain that the real system in question cannot be like the model of it, in important respects. Someone pursuing ergodic theory in statistical mechanics by examining the dynamics of colliding hard-sphere billiard balls is well aware that the real molecules that make up the gas are quite unlike such billiard balls in many irrelevant respects, say in their size or what they are made up out of. Beyond this there is an awareness, from the beginning, that even in the respects in which the model is being used to illuminate the behavior of the real system, the model is misrepresenting the real world as well. For even from the beginning of the kinetic theory it was expected that the dynamical forces between molecules would be better represented by a "soft" potential interaction than by the "hard," perfectly elastic and instantaneous, collisions that are introduced to characterize the billiard-ball collisions of the model.

In other cases, however, the model is, reasonably, thought of as representing "how things really are." Or, perhaps more conservatively and more plausibly, the model is being treated as a representation of the real system which, at the time, one has no definitive reason for thinking of as definitely not fully representative of how things are, or at least approximately, are. In this case one knows that one's description of the world has invoked idealizations. And one suspects that a rigorously true account of things may lead to results that, therefore, differ from the calculated consequences obtained by the idealizing, modeling, procedure. But one still thinks of the model as being a characterization of how things are that is not, as in the cases above, a clear *mis*representation in important respects.

It is tempting, perhaps, to think of the two cases as not really differing from one another at some deeper level. All scientific description, one may be inclined to think after seeing how often models of the first kind are employed in fundamental science, is some sort of metaphorical account of the world. Some of the claims that scientific assertions do not, and are not really intended to, treat of the real world, but only of models, may be leaning in this direction.

But such claims are, I believe, very dubious and probably incoherent. Without some grasp of the notion of what it is to offer a description of a system intended genuinely to characterize that system, and not just to characterize some other system thought of as standing in some kind of metaphorical relation to the real system, it is hard to understand what would count as any notion of "similarity" among systems, in particular what would count as making the model system in any way an appropriate metaphor for the real system. And such a notion of similarity is going to be essential to any account offered by those who take laws and theories as intended only to characterize models and not as intended to describe the world. For without the notion of similarity they cannot even begin to account for how our laws and theories are to be applied by us to the tasks of predicting and explaining the behavior of real systems. Laws and theories as free-floating as they would be if taken as descriptions of models and not of the world, and lacking any account of the relation of model to real system in the world, would be no better than components of some fictional story about any imagined world we choose to fantasize. Unless we understand some assertions as speaking to the actual nature of real systems, we are left without any grip on how some invocation of idealization and models is supposed to play a genuine scientific purpose. Whatever theories are, they are not merely metaphors.

But it is certainly true, as I have been at pains to emphasize, that our laws and theories only apply to the real world given significant amounts of idealization that have been built into the understanding of how the theories are to be applied. Accounting for the role such idealization plays in allowing us to develop rigorous, systematic theories that are nonetheless applicable to a messy world is, indeed, an important methodological task. It is a vital issue how treating systems as isolated when they really are not, treating theories as comprehensive when they are really only partial, and treating systems and processes as existing in limiting forms when the real systems and processes do not live at such limits, can play legitimate roles in our theory of the world.

I have argued that dealing with idealization methodologically is in some ways an easier, and in other ways a much harder, task than has sometimes been thought. In many cases of the use of idealized models in our theoretical accounts of the world the scientific community is, properly, quite relaxed about the deviations that may occur between idealized and real system or process. These are the cases where our scientific theory itself, either the theory in question or relevant presupposed background theory, gives us a strong grip on the consequences incurred by invoking our idealization. These are the cases where the idealization is controllable in one way or another. But in other cases there can be deep and fundamental disagreements about the very legitimacy of the idealization in question. Or there can be intractable problems in gaining an understanding of how to constrain the legitimate applications of the particular idealization.

In some cases the very understanding of the kind of theory one is dealing with and of the fundamental explanatory structure supposed to hold for the experiential domain in question may hinge upon the scientist's beliefs about which idealizations are to be taken as appropriate. In other cases, even when the legitimacy and nature of the idealization is not in question, the appropriate means for relating the idealized cases to the realistic cases may not be easily available. For a case of the former kind, think of the role played by the idealization of systems as isolated in the non-Machian and in the Machian theories of dynamics. Or, for another such case, think of the radically different roles played by the idealizations of infinite number of components and infinite time in the various antagonistic rationalizations of statistical mechanics. For a case of the latter type, think of the scientific difficulties that can be encountered when one wishes to integrate a number of partial theories in a domain where strong nonlinearities play an important role.

In dealing with both of these kinds of cases, what we discover in scientific practice is the need to combine modes of reasoning usually thought of as philosophical with resort to experimental data and to the best available scientific theories. It is this kind of complex, and context-dependent, thinking that constitutes theorizing at the foundational level. And it is in explorations of this kind, I believe, that we find by far the richest field for exploring the really important roles that idealization plays within fundamental theoretical science.

Suggested Readings

For a discussion of the romanticist attack on science see Abrams (1971). The idea of laws as inference rules of limited scope begins in Ramsey (1960) and Ryle (1950). An extended discussion of the implicit background against which explicit science takes place is Polanyi (1958). For general discussions of the laws of physics as fundamentally untrue to the world and of laws as applying directly only to models see Cartwright (1983) and chaps. 3 and 4 of Giere (1988). On phenomenological physics as opposed to theoretical description again see Cartwright (1983).

For a philosophical discussion of chaos theory and its implications for the notions of interference and controllability see Smith (1998). On Newtonian theory and its Machian critique see Barbour (1989), chap. III of Sklar (1974), and Earman (1989). On the alleged non-isolability of systems in thermodynamics see Blatt (1959), Mayer (1961), and sect. 7. III. 2 of Sklar (1993). Horwich (1987) offers an alternative anti-isolationist account of thermodynamic irreversibility.

On decoherence accounts of measurement in orthodox quantum mechanics see Omnès (1994). For the role of non-isolation in Bohm's interpretation of quantum mechanics see chap. 6 of Bohm and Hiley (1993). On the role of causality principles in quantum field theory and vanishing commutators at spacelike separations see chap. II of Visconti (1969). The cluster decomposition principle is in chap. 4 of Weinberg (1995).

On the decomposition of forces and its relevance see essay 3, pp. 54–73 of Cartwright (1983). For an introduction to structural stability see chap. 12 of Abraham and Shaw (1992). For a survey of issues in the reduction of thermodynamics to statistical mechanics see chap. 9 of Sklar (1993). The role of limiting procedures in thermodynamics and statistical mechanics are discussed in Ruelle (1969), Lebowitz (1983), and Lanford (1983). Philosophical discussions of the issues are in Sklar (1993).

For material on the role of limiting procedures in intertheoretic reduction see Malament (1986) and Rohrlich (1989) on the relation of relativistic spacetime to pre-relativistic spacetime. For material on the relation of quantum mechanics to pre-quantum theories see Rohrlich (1990). To get the flavor of some of the real difficulties that arise in relating classical to quantum physics see Part II of Ozorio de Almeida (1988) and Batterman (1997).

For models see chap. 3 of Giere (1988), Cartwright (1983), Redhead (1980), Laymon (1985), Hesse (1966), and Koperski (1998).

4

Transience

We have been exploring two general types of grounds for doubting that we ought to claim any simple kind of truth for our best available foundational physical theories. One group of arguments to this effect rested upon skepticism concerning the referential nature of our theories. It was suggested that one ought to be very wary of immediately assuming that, just because a theory apparently refers to some theoretical entity or property, such an entity or property must be truly needed in a correct description of the world. Reference to the in-principle unobservable was thought to be particularly suspicious in this way. The second group of arguments rested upon claims to the effect that our best available theories are never really true descriptions of the world. They are, it was claimed, at most true only in some idealized sense, or, perhaps more precisely, true only of idealized models that bear some kind of similarity relation to the real things of the world.

In both of these cases I argued that there is a very rich body of philosophically interesting issues to be explored. But, in both cases, I argued that by far the most interesting issues will be found in the detail of how the global, skeptical claims just outlined become particularized and concrete when they appear as specific problems about theories within the context of ongoing physical theorizing. When the issues of ontological elimination and idealization are examined in the role they play within ongoing science, they present a quite different aspect, and a much richer vein of problems, than they do when they are explored only as global, skeptical theses about science in general, abstracted from the messy details of their role within the science itself.

At this point I want to examine briefly similar sorts of issues that arise out of a third kind of skeptical doubt about the simple truth of our foundational theories. Not surprisingly, I will argue, as before, that a focus on the abstract and global issues that arise out of these skeptical considerations may prove less interesting and less illuminating than a detailed exploration of the issues that arise when this third kind of doubt is seen as working within the particular contexts of specific scientific problems.

How could anyone be so foolish as to believe in the truth of the best of our currently available foundational physical theories? Doesn't the whole history of science tell us that the reign of any allegedly fundamental theory is transient? Theories are constructed in order to do justice to the experimental data available at a time. But the pool of data a theory must deal with grows as instrumental abilities improve. Theories are framed utilizing the theory-framing devices, in particular the mathematics, currently available. But our means for framing ever-deeper and richer theoretical structures grows with the ever-increasing richness of the conceptual apparatus available to us.

There have been periods in the history of physics when scientists may very well have believed, and believed with some good reason, that they had finally found the stable, true theory of at least a portion of the world. Perhaps the first half of the eighteenth century constitutes such a period, at least as far as a portion of dynamics is concerned. But after the history of radical expansion, revision, and revolution that has constituted theoretical physics over the last centuries, isn't it the case that the only reasonable belief to hold is that our current best available theories are ultimately headed for the scrap-heap that has welcomed their predecessors?

There are reasons, though, other than this grand induction over the transience of past theories, that tend to convince us that we ought not to think of our current best available foundational theories as constituting a true stopping point in the course of radical scientific change. There are deep and pervasive aspects of our current fundamental theory that move nearly everyone in the scientific and methodological community to be quite skeptical that these theories constitute our final theory of the world. This is true despite periodic claims in the popular scientific press, claims often espoused by distinguished theoreticians who ought to know better, that the "final theory" is at hand.

Let me postpone for the moment saying what some of the specific reasons are for being skeptical of the finality of our present theory. Bringing them to the fore will play an important role later on. Suffice it to say for now that substantial reasons exist, both of a historical, metatheoretic kind (that is to say, the grand induction over past scientific failure), and of a kind more internal to the nature of our current best available theories and our evidence for them, that impel us to think it unreasonable to believe that our current theories will always be accepted as best available science. And, if that is true, substantial reasons exist that make it unreasonable now to claim truth for our current best available fundamental science.

Nor, therefore, ought we to believe in our current best theories. The claim that the statement "I believe p, but p isn't true" is some kind of contradiction, or at least some kind of conceptual incoherence, seems to be central to whatever we are talking about when we discuss the cognitive attitude we call belief. Systematically to deny truth to our best available fundamental theories, on the basis of general fallibilist arguments and on the basis of their own inner difficulties, and yet to claim that we ought to believe these theories, would seem to court incoherence.

But if we don't believe, and ought not to believe, the foundational theories, what cognitive attitude or attitudes do we hold, and ought we to hold, toward them? There are three basic questions that I would like to explore here. First, what is the range of cognitive attitudes that we find ourselves holding, or advocating others to hold, when the object of the attitudes is that part of science that constitutes our current foundational physical theories? Second, is there some way in which we can strengthen our cognitive attitude toward these theories by trading off the reinterpretation of the supposed cognitive content of the theories? Finally, can we discover some general structures in our best foundational theories to date which, when combined with philosophically motivated general principles, might help us frame the appropriate cognitive attitude toward specific components of our fundamental theory? This last issue will consist in part in exploring the question of how science itself can guide us to a way of acknowledging the transient nature of our currently best available theory while, without actually replacing the current theory with a theoretical alternative, finding appropriate ways of dealing here and now with its anticipated place in ongoing science, including the science of the future.

1. KINDS OF COGNITIVE ATTITUDES

If we do not believe, and ought not to believe, our best available foundational theories, then what cognitive attitude should we take towards them? There is a well-known move away from belief and toward a more subtle and complex scheme of cognitive attitudes that has proven both conceptually rich in its own right and enormously valuable in capturing many important aspects of our cognitive stances toward the world. This is the scheme of partial beliefs. In its most insightful and productive formalized version it becomes the system of subjective probabilities. If we ought not to believe our best available fundamental physical theories, ought we to have toward them a cognitive attitude framable as a partial belief and formalizable as a subjective probability?

Although the scheme of subjective probabilities has functioned so brilliantly in numerous contexts of analyzing cognitive attitudes and their changes in the light of new evidence, I do not think that it will do the job we need done in the present problem situation. There are numerous ways of formalizing notions of partial belief. These can include the full-fledged assignment of exact subjective probabilities to assertions, or they can be weaker systems, as in the schemes where we only partially order propositions ordinally with respect to believability or where convex sets of subjective probabilities, rather than specific values, are used to characterize our cognitive attitude toward a proposition.

A basic framework underlying all of these approaches is the idea that we are presented with a collection of propositions one of which we take to be true. In the neatest cases the propositions are incompatible with one another and so only one can be true; that is, the propositions form an exhaustive and exclusive set. But we don't know which of the propositions really is true. Systems of subjective probabilities, and their variants, show us that there is a rich theory of rationality in which we can frame our cognitive stance toward the members of such a set of propositions. This will provide a canon of rational belief and of rational action that will allow us to believe and act in ways that are subject to various plausible constraints of reason, even if we don't know which of the propositions is the true one.

We can, for example, demand principles that prevent us from violating transitivity for the notion of comparative believability. We will, then, never end up being more confident of the truth of A than we are of the truth of B, more confident of B than of C, yet more confident of C than of A. With a number of additional, and problematic, posits, we can show that such a system of ordered believability can be represented by a numerical assignment of "degrees of probability" to the proposition, where the numerical assignments obey the formal rules of the theory of probability. Alternatively, and more commonly, the grounding for the assignment of subjective probabilities is rationalized by tying together cognitive attitudes toward actions, especially actions in the face of risk. Once again principles of rationality are posited, only now they are principles regulating classes of possible actions. We might demand that our partial beliefs be such that we cannot be enticed into a combination of bets that enforce a loss on us, or, more weakly, that let us lose but prevent us from winning. Or, more deeply, we can impose requirements of transitivity, and other constraints of detail, on our preferences among lotteries offered to us. From these posits we are able to derive conclusions about the representation of partial beliefs, and, in the deeper versions, representations of desires as well. From this comes a theory of subjective probability, since the numerical representations of the beliefs can be shown to obey the standard axioms of mathematical probability. In the deeper proofs we obtain a representation result for the subjective utilities as well. But here, once again, the basic assumption is that, of all the possible states of the world under consideration, one of them is the actual world.

In a number of methodological contexts in the philosophy of

science subjective probability theory has proven an interesting and suggestive framework for at least partially understanding some long-abiding puzzles. If we make the fundamental assumption that one ought to update one's present subjective probabilities in the light of new evidence by the rule of conditionalization, or by one of its variants such as Jeffrey conditionalization, we can formulate a theory of probabilistic confirmation of hypotheses by data. From this perspective important insight can be gained into such issues as the positive role played by variety of evidence in confirmation. Insight can also be gained into what was once called enumerative induction. Other insights enlighten us about the roles generality and systematic power play in the practice of theory choice.

Whether such so-called Bayesian inference techniques tell us all there is to know about confirmation of theories in science is another matter. Approaches utilizing subjective probability are fundamentally concerned with allocating degrees of confidence amongst a number of candidates for the truth. We think one of the alternatives before us is true; we just don't know which. But in the situation with which we are concerned we are quite convinced that none of the present best available theories we are considering can be reasonably considered to be true. Indeed, we are quite certain that our current best theory is false. The question before us is, then, what cognitive attitude we should take toward such theories, given that believing, or even having some "partial belief," in a theory we know to be false seems incoherent.

We need some more complex sorts of cognitive attitudes than can be found in notions such as belief or in partial belief understood as some kind of degree of confidence. The most obvious mechanism for framing such more complex cognitive attitudes is the invocation of second-order beliefs about the theory. It will no longer be a question of believing or disbelieving or having some confidence in the theory. It will be a matter, rather, of believing something or other to be the case about the theory, the "something or other" not being truth or falsity.

In another context, one closely related to our first topic of ontological elimination, use has been made of such second-order beliefs in the doctrine of "constructive empiricism." In order to get around the underdetermination problem, the problem that the totality of empirical data will always remain compatible with a plurality of apparently alternative theories that differ from one another in what they say about the realm of the unobservable, some traditional empiricisms took all such alternative theories as really saying the same thing. They reduced the asserted content of each of the theories to what it said about the observables. This constitutes, perhaps, a radical version of a "content-thinning" approach to resolving the problem. Constructive empiricism, however, takes the apparent assertive differences between the theories to be real differences of content. But it proposes to alleviate our skeptical concerns by suggesting to us that science does not, and ought not to, decide which theory we ought to believe. The aim of science is, rather, to tell us which theories we ought to "accept as empirically adequate." That is, the aim of science is to tell us when to believe that a theory correctly predicts the totality of observational facts. If we have such a second-order belief about one of the theories in a set that are all observationally equivalent to one another, then we ought, perforce, to have the same second-order belief about any of the alternative accounts in the set. The job of choosing among the alternatives, then, is no job at all. For choosing any one of the alternatives will be perfectly acceptable.

Constructive empiricism is introduced here only to provide a familiar example of dealing with a problem by moving from "belief" to "belief about" of a particular kind. The notion of empirical adequacy will plainly not help with the problem that is our current focus of attention. For the reasons, both those that are particular and those that follow from the grand induction over past transience of theories, that lead us to think our current theories won't be acceptable in the future, are reasons for us to think that the theories won't be empirically adequate in the future either.

One option for dealing with the problem of transience is to assert that our cognitive attitudes toward theories in science ought to look only at the past and present. We ought not to worry about what the future will bring, but only about what the past and present have brought us. Here is one version of such a proposal: What we ought to do is to compare our present best available theories with respect to all those alternative candidate theories that have preceded it or that have been proposed contemporaneously with it. Then we ought to formulate the ways in which we think our presently accepted theory is superior to its rejected predecessors or contemporaries, and we ought to express our cognitive attitude toward the selected theory as a belief that it is superior to the alternatives available in just those respects.

Now making the comparisons we need to make between our current theory and the possible alternative to it may be problematic. There will be those, for example, who tell us that the theories are often so different from one another in their conceptual frameworks that the assertions of one such theory cannot even be taken as semantically comparable to those of any of the others. Such allegations of "radical incommensurability" have led some to various kinds of skepticism about there being any kind of rational process for comparatively evaluating alternative foundational theoretical accounts. Others have accepted the thesis of radical incommensurability and proposed evaluation procedures that rely only on methods that evaluate each of the competitors by means internal to its own world picture.

I am dubious that any such "internalist" methods will provide all the resources we need for the full theory-comparison task. But I am also very dubious of the dramatic claims of radical incommensurability. If we adopt a quick and facile doctrine of meaning holism, one in which the meaning of a term varies with any change in the body of assertions involving that term, and certain quick ideas about how meaning is involved in the logical interrelations among propositions involving terms with the meanings in question, then what follows is a radical inability to logically relate assertions that exist in any two theories that disagree with one another in any respect. And adopting these doctrines will further lead to the rather bizarre consequence that one denies the possibility of disagreement ever existing between two speakers. For on the terms of such a theory of meaning and entailment, the very disagreement between the speakers guarantees that in denying each other's claims they must be equivocating on the meaning of the terms and actually talking past one another. What that shows us, I think, is that the notions of meaning holism and logical relation adopted were, indeed, too quick and facile to provide us with any useful clarification of the notions of meaning and of logical entailment.

We do not, of course, have any theory of meaning that will really do justice to the issue of meaning invariance through theoretical change. It does seem quite clear, however, that there are explicable meaning relations between the concepts of theories, even between the concepts of theories that differ from one another in quite fundamental ways. While the radical meaning holists have pointed out to us the need for a much deeper inquiry than there has yet been into the way in which meaning relationships survive conceptual change, their skeptical doubts are no reason for despair. Somehow or another sufficient logical connections do hold through changes in asserted content that communication between those who don't agree on all the facts of the world remains possible.

One thing we can do, then, is to look at our best available theory in some domain and compare it in various respects, empirical or theoretical, with its past and present competitors. We can ask if it betters them in empirical adequacy, say, or in the economy or the simplicity of its domain of ontological posits. We can then express our preferential attitude for the chosen theory, not as belief in its truth, but as belief in its superiority in some respects or other compared to its past and present contenders. Such comparison of a theory with its predecessors and its contemporaries is, surely, the core of the process we undertake when we decide in which theory to place our current confidence, such as that confidence is. Here we need only reflect on all the work in methodology, epistemology, confirmation theory, and decision theory that impels us to think of hypothesis acceptance as being the selection of one or more preferred hypotheses from a designated class of alternative hypotheses. What could such a reference class be if it is not all of the viable competitors so far thought of by our scientific imagination? A number of reliabilist accounts of knowledge, for example, propose referring to a class of designated viable alternatives, using such a reference class to undercut some varieties of radical skepticism. If we are going to choose some hypothesis in science as the preferred hypothesis, it seems clear that the preference can only be relative to the alternative hypotheses available from past and current theorizing.

But have we said everything there is to say about our cognitive attitude toward our current preferred hypotheses when we have pointed out the ways in which we find them superior to their current best available contenders? I don't think so. For those considerations will not, by themselves, tell us the degree to which we think the current best theory is "getting at the truth." We could believe a theory to be preferable to all of its current competitors, and yet not believe it to be in any way an indicator of "how things really are." Indeed, some philosophers, emphasizing the way in which theory choice takes place in a context relativized to a current comparison class of alternatives, would have us eschew any reference to "aiming at the truth" as one of the ends of science at all.

But, I believe, the naive idea of truth as the aim, or at least one of the aims, of scientific theorizing is the correct idea, and I think that we can say a good deal more about how this idea of aiming at the truth plays out in our scientific method. In particular we can, I think, say much more about how we may try to reconcile the claims that our ideal cognitive attitude toward a theory would be to believe it, that is, to believe it to be true, with our fallibilist conviction that none of our best available theories have been or are worthy of such epistemic esteem.

In order to frame the kind of cognitive attitude we do, and ought to, take toward our current theories, if belief won't do, what we need to do is something that will appeal to the naive intuition of the working scientist. We need to ask what we believe, now, about what will be the status of our current best theories in the future. We cannot now, of course, say what our future accepted scientific hypotheses will be, for if we could they wouldn't be the future hypotheses but the current ones. We can, however, now frame beliefs about what we will, in the future, take to be the status of our current best available theories. We don't believe, now, that in the future we will believe our current best available theories to be true. But we may very well believe now, and with good reasons, that we are entitled, now, to believe of our current theories that they are "on the road to truth" and that in the future they will be looked upon as having "been headed in the right direction."

As I said, I think that this is often the naive view of the philosophically unsophisticated working scientist. But being the belief held by the naive is not in itself a mark of falsehood. Despite all the claims that have been made as to the radical nature of scientific revolutions and the framework shifts they bring with them, and despite all the claims—historicized Kantian, pragmatist, deconstructionist, or whatever—to the effect that our science is at best relative to some conceptual background itself not rooted in the nature of the world but in some sense arbitrary or conventional, there is good reason, I think, to accept the scientists' conviction that the bulk of our current theory will have a permanent place in science, if not as the truth, then as an appropriate stage of science on the road to the truth. But saying what that might mean is, of course, very problematic.

A natural first move is to try and characterize our epistemic attitude toward our current theory as a belief that the current theory is, if not true, at least approximately true. But that won't do. First off, we discover that saying what it is for a theory to be approximately true is a very difficult task. In certain simple cases, where, for example, a theory takes the form of predicting the numerical value for one parameter as a function of the numerical values of some set of other parameters, the usual notions of approximation in terms of magnitude of error or fractional extent of error may do the trick. But it is difficult even to imagine what a general notion of approximation might even mean that would enable us to speak of one theory as being some kind of "conceptual approximation" to a theory that differs from it in aspects of conceptual structure.

Here again a natural, instinctive response comes to mind. Why not restrict one's attention to the observational predictions of a theory, and take our attitude to be only that our current best available theory ought to be believed approximately true in its observational predictions? There will be those, of course, who will deny that we can even make sense of any cross-theoretical notion of the observational predictions of theories, but let us put such radical, and I think implausible, versions of the doctrine of incommensurability to the side. But even if we do so, we cannot have much confidence that moving to the notion of approximate truth, and restricting its domain of application to the observational predictions of the theory, will really give us the notions we want when we wish to know what cognitive attitude we ought to take toward our current best theory. The notion that we ought to believe our theories as being merely approximately true with regard to their observational predictions is both too strong and too weak to capture what our cognitive attitude toward them really ought to be.

It is too strong, since we can quite easily be convinced that our current best theories are probably not going to be approximately in accordance with our future theories even in those of their consequences that are taken to be observational in some strictly construed sense. There will almost certainly always be physical conditions realizable by experiment in which our current best theories give us totally wrong predictions about the observations that will be obtained. It is, however, reasonable to suspect that there will be large domains of physical conditions for which our current preferred theories will serve as reasonably reliable predictors of observational outcomes, even into the perpetual future. If there were not, we would never have accepted them in the first place. The problem is that we will usually not be able, now, to specify what the domain of perpetual reliable observational prediction of our current theory will be. That is because the conditions under which our current best theory will radically fail in its observational predictions will usually be revealed to us not by the present theory, but by its as yet unknown successor. Prerelativistically, for example, it wouldn't have occurred to those immersed in Newtonian science that Newtonian dynamics would radically fail in its observational reliability when velocities of material objects neared that of light. It remains true, nonetheless, that part of our appropriate cognitive attitude toward our best current theories is the belief that, come what may in future science, there is at least some domain of physical situations for which the current theory will remain a reliable predictor of observational outcomes into the perpetual future. But, of course, the limits of that domain may be quite impenetrable to us. There is much to be said in favor of the widely held view that what was once proper scientific belief can remain as a good guide to engineering process even when the theoretical science no longer survives as believable theory.

To characterize our cognitive attitude as merely believing our theories approximately true at the observational level is too weak to capture the notion in ways that are even more interesting and important. What scientists often really believe, and it may be argued what they ought to believe, is that the best currently available theory is "heading in the right direction" even at the highest levels of its posited theoretical apparatus.

Indeed, it is hard to see how one could have any confidence in the ultimate predictive accuracy of a theory, even as only an approximate predictor over a limited domain of the observational phenomena, without having some degree of confidence that, one way or another, the theoretical apparatus of the theory must be "pointing toward the truth" as well. For, as has often been remarked, it would be nothing short of miraculous that our current best theories are as accurate as they are over such vast domains of empirical phenomena were there not *something* about their theoretical postulations that somehow corresponded to something in the world. This is true even if the theories are, as we know, not the end products of our ultimate science and even if they wear their future dismissal from the ranks of the accepted hypotheses on their sleeves.

And this claim about what the cognitive status of the theoretical posits of our current science is and ought to be can be sustained even in the face of the familiar examples trotted out by those who would dismiss truth as an aim of science altogether. These examples are the notorious cases of past theories that seemed to work quite well as approximate predictors in moderately extensive domains of observable phenomena, but that were, allegedly, later discarded by science as "altogether wrong-headed" in their posits at the theoretical level. According to some, examples of this kind were the theories of the crystalline spheres on ancient astronomy, the phlogiston theory of combustion, and the substantival caloric theory of heat.

There are a number of responses that can be offered to the claim that such examples show it to be unreasonable of science to think of its current theoretical beliefs even as "heading in the right direction." First, it isn't at all clear that one ought to think of the standard examples of such rejected theories as "totally wrong-headed" in the light of the theories that succeeded them. Careful reflection on the cases will show them as having more truth to themselves at the theoretical level, as evaluated in the light of later science, than appears at first glance. This is so even if some of their theoretical conceptions must, in the light of what succeeded them, be admitted to be very wrong indeed. Second, there are the well-known arguments to the effect that "that was then and this is now." That is, even if many of the "crude" theories accepted in earlier science turned out to be utterly wrong-headed, it might still be the case that we, now, have good reason to think that the best theories of our current "mature" fundamental physics must have much more going for them in the long run than did such leaps in the dark as the theories of crystalline spheres, phlogiston, or caloric. Finally, and most importantly, what we wish to understand is what the cognitive attitude of scientists is and ought to be toward their contemporary theories. It may very well be that they believe them to be "heading in the right direction" at the theoretical level and that it is reasonable for them to do so, even if it sometimes turns out to be the case that such a cognitive attitude toward their best theories is wrong.

In the light of the internal and empirical difficulties faced by our best current theories, then, and in the light of the general induction from past scientific revolutions, we may very well wish to deny that we believe in our current best theories or that we are willing, when pressed, to assert their truth. But we may very well be willing to believe that they are "heading toward the truth" or "pointing to the truth," and we may be willing to assert their future status as appropriate historical stages in the process of developing a true theory of the world. This is, of course, something that will sound truistic to most philosophically naive practicing scientists. And it will almost assuredly sound outrageously naive to many philosophers enthralled by notions of the radicalness of scientific revolutions, impressed as they are by the strong incompatibility in asserted content between predecessor and successor theories in such revolutions, and even insistent that the radical incommensurability of their concepts makes them not even comparable with regard to degree of truth. But that doesn't make the scientists wrong and those philosophers right.

But what does "heading in the right direction" mean here? I doubt that any general characterization can be formulated of what it is for a theory to be pointing us in the right direction in its theoretical conceptualization of the world. Or, rather, I doubt that there is much one can say at this level that will be informatively rich in analytic content. It is conceivable that some very general and very abstract formal notions could be formulated of the way in which the concepts of one theory are related to those of another, in particular to those of a successor theory. And such formal notions might be of use in explaining what it is for the conceptualization of the later theory to be a "later stage" of a process in which the earlier theory was a stage. That is, one might be able to say in some very abstract and general ways what the relations might be between the concepts of the theories that make the concepts of the successor theory a progressive improvement on those of its predecessor. The sort of concepts that Sneed presents in his discussion of theory change from a Ramsey sentence perspective on the structure of theories is the sort of thing that might be useful here. But one would be hard put to find anything rich enough that is framable in so very abstract a manner and that would make it clear to us just what is being insisted upon by scientists when they claim that there is a progressive evolution of concepts in our fundamental theory as predecessors give way to their successors.

Yet the claim that such meaning relationships often exist between the theoretical structures of one theory and that of the theory that follows it, and the claim that these relations are such as to justify our claiming, in retrospect, that the earlier theory could be considered a stage in an evolutionary progression of theories of which the later theory was the next stage, are both claims that are plausibly supported by the history of fundamental theories in physics. Here, again, I think that gaining any insights into what these meaning relationships might be like, and into how such evolutionary conceptual changes take place, will require delving into specific cases. It is there that many of the richest insights are to be obtained. We will touch on these issues again shortly.

Perhaps the most we can do at the level of highest abstraction is to make a number of broad, and mostly negative, assertions. First, making the claim that such conceptual evolution exists is, of course, an implicit rejection of any thesis of radical incommensurability between the concepts of the theories that follow one another in the historical succession of science. It is hard to imagine how one could express the way in which the concepts of a current theory are "pointing" toward the concepts of its successor if there were no way whatever to construe meaning relationships between the concepts of the two theories. But radical incommensurability was never a plausible thesis to begin with. Granted, we have no account of meaning that will tell us all that we want to say about the relationships between terms that are defined by their roles in theories and that function in distinct total bodies of asserted content. But to espouse a meaning holism so radical as to imply the impossibility of two speakers ever contradicting one another is to reject any hope for an understanding of meaning altogether.

To maintain that the theories at one time, although ultimately to be replaced by successors incompatible with them, are leading us in the right direction, is also to deny that the temporal sequence of our scientific theories is radically arbitrary. It would be foolhardy to claim that the evolution of our scientific understanding of the world had to follow the exact course that it did, or to claim that there is an inevitability in all of the details of its actual progress. No doubt some discoveries in science, even some broad theoretical conceptualizations of it, even those at the level of fundamental physics, might have been made in ways that differ from the historical pattern these discoveries actually followed. But there is much to be said for the scientist's naive belief that such adventitiousness in the historical order of discovery could amount only to minor possibilities of things happening differently than they actually did in the evolution of scientific understanding. How we discover the inner workings of nature is dependent on what nature really is like, and is dependent on what we are like as interpreters of it. A plausible case can be made to the effect that, given the constraints imposed on the evolution of scientific understanding by the way both nature and we are made up, the broad outlines of the order of discovery in science, of the order of theoretical understanding, refinement, and progress, has a fair degree of inevitability to it.

It is also true that there is much to be said for the claim of the philosophically naive scientist that the theories and their successors, so far from being incommensurable with one another, share deep and important conceptual similarities even at their most fundamental theoretical levels. There is in such a claim, of course, no denial that revolutionary changes occur in our fundamental theories. Nor is there any attempt to deny that novel foundational theories often bring with them astonishing conceptual surprises. New theories often treat of the world in ways wholly unforeseen, and probably unforeseeable, in terms of the science that preceded them. But all of that is perfectly compatible with the claim that, revolutionary differences between predecessor and successor theory notwithstanding, the theories inevitably bear deep conceptual relationships to one another at the level of their most abstract and most theoretical concepts. The historical progression of foundational physical theories, it can be argued, is one that, with some exceptions, shows an order of theories in which each successor theory is framed in concepts that are refinements and deepenings of the concepts of the theory that preceded it. Indeed, it is almost impossible to imagine how one could ever arrive at the kind of profound theories that now form the foundations of physics unless it were by such an evolutionary process. Revolutionary as many of the changes of theory have been, the newer theory never springs full-blown and *ex nihilo* from the mind of the theoretician unencumbered by a need to understand how to get to the new stage in theorizing by some modification or other of what went before.

If this general perspective on the dynamic history of the changes in foundational theories is correct, then it makes good sense to say that, although we can't rationally believe our current best theories to be true, we can certainly believe them to be "pointing toward the truth" and can believe them to be "stages along the road to the truth." But leaving things at that level will once more miss the main point. That point is that merely having such a global perspective on transience, and on the implications of transience for the appropriateness of the cognitive attitudes we do and ought to take toward our fundamental theories, will overlook a rich body of insight to be obtained when one asks a different sort of question. This is the question: How, within the ongoing practice of theory construction, critique, and revision, does working science itself deal internally with the contextually dependent need to do something in the present in response to a present realization that one's current best theory is at best a transient occupant in that preferred position?

2. THINNING CONTENT

Shortly, I will return to my central theme of arguing from cases that the exploration of such issues as the transient lifetime of even our best current theories becomes a much richer field of inquiry when discussed within the context of their specific appearances in particular scientific programs, rather than being pursued in a theory-independent and context-free manner. But here I want briefly to violate my own principles by making a few remarks about one more traditional and context-free way of dealing with the issue of transience. The results obtained will be, not surprisingly, rather thin, but they are perhaps worth a moment's attention.

We are inclined to deny that we believe in, or are prepared to assert the truth of, our best contemporary theories, since we believe that they will be replaced in our epistemic esteem in the future by alternative accounts that are incompatible with them, even if those future replacement theories are now beyond our ken. One way of dealing with this problem, I have suggested, is to move to a weaker kind of cognitive attitude toward our best contemporary theories than the attitude of belief. Instead of believing in the current best theories, we ought to adopt some kind of second-order belief about them. And I have suggested that one plausible sort of such a weaker cognitive stance is to believe that our current best theories are the best current candidates for the role of pointing to future truth. That is, we ought to believe our best available theories to be the best stages available in the evolutionary progress of scientific theories to be continued into the future.

There is, however, another way of dealing with the problems that arise from our belief in the transience of theories. I earlier briefly noted this alternative approach as it is applied in another context. When discussing the inexactness of our theories when applied to real systems, I noted that one move that could be made to restore truth to the scientific assertions would be to interpret those assertions in a more flexible manner. Instead of claiming, for example, that certain parameters of a system would have a specific, exact numerical value, we may interpret the scientific claim as merely asserting that the value of the parameter, for the real system and not some model of it, would be within some specified range of the theoretically exact parameter value. So to restore truth, we can reduce the pretensions of our assertion, that is, thin down the assertion's intended semantic content.

Couldn't we apply such a general move in the present context of the problems raised by the transience of theories, as well? Instead of weakening our cognitive attitude toward our current best theories away from full belief, why not, instead, thin down what we take to be the asserted content of these theories and adopt an attitude of full belief to the now weaker assertions?

Suppose, for example, that in our future science we were to come to the conclusion that we should deny the existence of a material world altogether and, instead, adopt some version or other of a totally idealist world picture. This may seem a pretty silly possibility to contemplate, but, after all, Leibnizian and Berkeleian idealism do still retain the powerful philosophical impetus that motivated them in the first place. In addition, and more relevantly for our purposes, it isn't as though dualist, or even pure idealist, metaphysical positions have been unknown as putative solutions to current deep problems in the interpretation of fundamental physics. These idealist proposals are motivated not by purely philosophical considerations but by experimental and physically theoretical considerations as well. Consider, for example, some of the idealist aspects of moves by Bohr, by Wigner, or by Albert and Loewer in their attempts at resolving the measurement problem in quantum mechanics.

Were our future science to tell us that we ought to believe in the existence only of minds and their contents and not in the existence of matter, what would that tell us about what our cognitive attitude toward the theory of, say, plate tectonics ought to be? Very little, I think. But how could that be? Doesn't the theory of plate tectonics deal with moving masses of the earth's crust? And isn't that crust presupposed to be a part of the material universe? If, then, we no longer believed in the existence of any matter at all, how could we possibly rationally go on espousing the theory of plate tectonics or believing in it?

The answer seems clear. Even if we no longer believed in matter, but, perhaps, only in "ideas in the mind" or "monads" or "well-founded phenomena," we could and would still hold on to many of the "smaller" theories we had constructed earlier on the basis of the presupposition that matter existed. We could and would do this simply by reconstruing these local theories in the new metaphysical terms. Whether the earth's crust is a portion of a really existing material world or, instead, nothing but a systematically correlated collection of ideas in minds, the issue of whether or not plate tectonics gives a correct account of the dynamical changes in the earth's crustal features remains unaffected.

There are many ways in which this point can be put. One could think of the choice of a theory such as the theory of plate tectonics as being a choice made relative to a specific collection of theory alternatives. All of the hypotheses in the set of alternatives from which we must choose one hypothesis as preferred may seem to make a common grand presupposition. The truth of such a presupposition is not in question when the issue is choosing one preferred hypothesis from the set. Should our basic presuppositions change, they would change uniformly for all of the members of the choice set. The preferability of one of the members of the set relative to its contenders, though, would remain invariant over the change of the presupposition.

Here is another way of putting the matter. We could argue that when we assert the theory of plate tectonics, or when we claim to believe it, what we are really asserting, and what our cognitive attitude of belief is really directed toward as its content, is a "thinner" content of the assertion than may appear to be the case at first. That is, the content of the theoretical hypothesis relevant to our assertions and beliefs is only that content of it that differentiates it in informational content from the alternative hypotheses of the choice set postulated above. Any part of its meaning that adverts to the physical or metaphysical presuppositions it makes and that it shares with the other hypotheses in the choice set are irrelevant in the theoretical choice situation. We can think of any such superfluous content as being "in suspension" when what is in question is the point of the scientific assertion made by expressing the hypothesis or the point of believing it to be true *qua* scientific hypothesis.

This way of dealing with the appropriate cognitive attitude to maintain in the face of transience may remind one of some of the claims made for context relativity when attributions of knowledge and questions of the reliability of methods are being discussed in traditional epistemology. When we claim to know that a building is a barn, it is alleged, we are claiming to have reliable indicators that it is not a house or a church, perhaps. In ordinary circumstances we are not claiming, for example, that we have reliable evidence that it is not an elaborate hologram or perhaps an image induced by direct electrical manipulation of our vatted brains by some malevolent neurologist.

The method of dealing with transience by thinning content of what is asserted may also remind one of the old debates about whether or not we ought to say that tables exist, in the light of our new physical knowledge about just how different the things we called tables are in reality from the way we thought they were in our everyday experience of them. Here letting the attributed content of an assertion such as "There is a table in this room" vary with the context of the use of that assertion may allow us to do justice to our intuition that we were both in one sense always right about tables, and in another sense very wrong indeed about what we thought about them. Allowing for a reduced content to some of our assertions, or, more generally, allowing for a content which is thinner or thicker depending upon the context in which the assertion is made, will allow us to say everything we want to say in such cases without worrying about multiplying entities in bizarre ways, say by having "ordinary" and "scientific" tables.

As noted earlier, reflecting on this possibility of thinning the content of our assertion may also throw some light on why some philosophers have maintained that, whereas the fundamental laws and theories posited by our science must all be denied truth, we can still affirm truth for the "surface" or "phenomenological" claims made in the course of science. Isn't it really the case that the latter kinds of assertions obtain their immunity to the kinds of skeptical doubts that lead these philosophers to deny truth to the deeper assertions, merely from the fact that they have very thin, and indeed variably thin, implicit asserted contents? It is easier to be right the less you claim about the world.

I will be the first to admit, however, that this notion of holding on to beliefs in the face of deep scientific change, or of affirming belief in our current theories even in the light of our expectation of such radical change in the future, by thinning the contents of our current most favorite assertions, really doesn't lead to much in the way of interesting philosophical exploration. It is indeed sensible to maintain that the theory of plate tectonics stands or falls with what happens in geological science, and not with what happens at the level of deep physical metaphysics. But much more insight can be gained into the scientific consequences of the realization of transience when we explore how science responds, in context and in ways determined by the specifics of the worries about transience, to the recognition that our current best theory is at best only a transient placeholder in the evolutionary progress of theories. It is to that issue that I now turn.

3. DEALING WITH TRANSIENCE WITHIN SCIENCE

Scientists don't worry very much about the fact that, on the basis of the "grand induction" from the failures of theories in past science, the present best available fundamental theory is just one more theory not likely to survive into the perpetual future as the permanently most preferred account of the world. Or, rather, such worries only occur to working scientists when they become engaged in the kind of extracurricular activity that has become so common of late in the form of numerous popular books speculating upon the possibility that the "final theory" is now in view.

When we discussed the issues of ontological elimination we observed that particular scientific projects of eliminating some range or other of the unobservables posited by current theory in some version of a reinterpretive program were never motivated by general operationalist, instrumentalist, or phenomenalist considerations alone. There was always some particular problematic aspect in current theory that was proving troublesome and that suggested the possibility that an eliminative reinterpretation of the theory might play a constructive role in the science of the time. Here, similarly, we discover that the real worries that occupy theoreticians about the tentative and transient nature of their current best theories are those that are generated by specific scientific difficulties with those theories, difficulties arising out of the contemporary experimental and theoretical situations. I set out below some of the kinds of difficulties that can motivate a scientist to withhold full backing from a current best theory and to believe that the theory is not the final goal of the scientific quest but only a stepping stone in that direction. Many of these sorts of difficulties have been noted in the past by methodologists.

(1) A current best theory may be confronted with experimental facts that seem to be incompatible with its observational predictions. Such "empirical anomalies," it has sometimes been suggested, are, indeed, always present, no matter how basically satisfactory our current best theory may seem to be to us. Of course, one might try to explain away the apparent contradiction between the data of experiments and the predictions of the theory in many ways. One could posit the existence of experimental error. Or one could blame the anomalous prediction on some implicit assumption needed to derive the contradictory prediction from one's theory, an assumption taken from the body of background science outside the theory in question. In one or other of these ways it might be possible to save the theory under investigation from revision in the face of the apparently fatal error of making an incorrect prediction about what will be observed. But such exculpatory moves can only be pushed

so far. At some point one may be forced on the basis of the data to withhold belief from the current best theoretical candidate, and be forced to admit that the theory is only a transient step on the road to some better theory.

(2) There may be a range of phenomena that one believes ought to be encompassable within a "completed" version of the current best theory, but which is not actually accounted for by the theory. Generally we won't expect any single theory to do justice to all of the observational and experimental facts about the world that are in need of explanation. But there will be cases where one has good reason to think that one's best available theory, a theory designed to account for the facts in some domain of observational experience, ought to be able to deal with some related observational facts as well, even though the theory appears unable to handle this extended range of observational phenomena. One becomes convinced that the current theory has not yet obtained its best, "most complete," final form. As an example, think of Einstein's desire to generalize from the theory of general relativity, which offered a geometric account of gravitation, in order to formulate a unified field theory that would geometrize electromagnetism as well.

(3) The best available candidates we now have for our fundamental theories of the world may be replete with internal formal and conceptual difficulties. This is hardly a novel situation in the history of science. To take but two examples, Newtonian dynamics had all the conceptual anomalies of the absolute reference frame to contend with, in particular its "in-principle unobservable" aspects. And classical electromagnetism was never able to formulate a fully satisfactory account that handled the divergence of a field at its origin in a point particle and was, hence, never fully adequate to formulating the theory of the interaction of a point charge with its own field. It was, therefore, never able to deal fully with radiation reaction.

Our current best fundamental theories are laden with such internal conceptual and formal difficulties. The general theory of relativity requires that many realistic physical situations result in the formation of spacetime singularities, giving rise to physical situations that, on the theory's own account, amount to a breakdown in the theory's ability to fully characterize its own domain of application. Quantum mechanics gives rise to the measurement problem, in which it appears that the theory requires in its own fundamental assumptions a characterization of processes in which systems are alleged to behave in a manner that is, on the basis of the theory's other fundamental postulates, physically impossible. Quantum field theory is infected with divergences in its formal predictions for observable quantities. These must be "controlled" in manners that often seem *ad hoc* and imported into the theory as saving devices that are difficult to understand within the theory's own conceptual framework. In the axiomatic versions of quantum field theory, designed in part to see if a formalization of the theory could evade some of the known internal conceptual anomalies, other internal formal difficulties appear that make its application to its paradigm problem cases puzzling. There is, for example, Haag's Theorem noted earlier that leads to puzzles in the rigorous treatment of scattering.

There is, in fact, a multiplicity of kinds of such internal conceptual and formal difficulties with theories. It would be quite a task to try and give an exhaustive taxonomy of them. But we can list a few that come quickly to mind.

(a) There may be a presence within a theory of conceptual problems that appear to be the result of mathematical artifacts. These seem to the theoretician to be not fundamental problems rooted in some deep physical mistake in the theory, but, rather, the consequence of some misfortune in the way in which the theory has been expressed. Haag's Theorem is, perhaps, a difficulty of this kind.

(b) There may be difficulties that arise when one needs to apply an otherwise well-behaved theory in some limiting situation. Difficulties of this kind might include, in different ways, the problem of dealing with the divergence of the electromagnetic field at its point of origin and the problem of the failure of general relativity at the very singularities whose existence it demands.

(c) There may be difficulties of the kind discussed in detail earlier, in which the theory suffers internal structural problems because it is possessed of an over-rich theoretical structure. The problems arising out of Newton's postulation of absolute space are of this kind.

(d) There may be internal conceptual problems that arise out of difficulties encountered in connecting the formal apparatus of the theory to its desired use in the prediction of observable phenomena. These might be called internal interpretive difficulties. The problem of fitting the measurement process in quantum mechanics into the remaining dynamical aspects of the theory is an internal conceptual problem of this kind.

The appearance of such internal conceptual difficulties in a theory is usually taken as a clear indication that it would not be reasonable to adopt a simple cognitive stance of belief toward such a theory. Instead, the prudent action would be to think of the theory as, again, merely a temporary stop-gap on the way to a better account of the phenomena. But much more importantly, the appearance of such internal conceptual anomalies in theories is often taken as strong motivation for beginning a systematic, future-looking program that anticipates the revision of the current best theory. This may very well include, of course, simply looking for a better theory to replace the existing one that is giving rise to the problems. But, as we shall see, it might mean engaging in something rather different, something preliminary to actually trying to construct the appropriate successor theory. It might mean, instead, taking on the task of asking what one can do, here and now, with the best available theory, in order to prepare the way for its hoped-for and anticipated future theoretical replacement.

(4) Finally, there may be a conceptual incompatibility between two or more of our best available fundamental theories, so that they cannot be taken as fitting together into a scientific whole. This may

be the case even if each of the theories requires that there be such a unification as a consequence of its internal structure. A currently important example of this kind is the incompatibility of our current best theory of gravity, the general theory of relativity, and the quantum-mechanical conceptualization of the general theory of states and their dynamics. General relativity, being a completely nonquantum theory, ignores entirely the radical revisions in ontology and ideology required by a quantum account of the world. But the quantum theory has as part of its content an implicit claim to universality. If quantum theory is correct then all of the features of the world must conform to its basic descriptive, kinematic, and dynamic constraints. Various arguments of detail also clearly indicate the impossibility of maintaining a world picture that is quantized in general but in which gravity, and spacetime itself, remain outside the quantum scheme. For this reason it has become a major project of contemporary physics to find the replacement for general relativity that will conform to the demands of quantum mechanics.

What I will be claiming, once again, is that there is a significant scientific project to be carried out that is distinct from the ultimate project of actually finding the new theory that resolves the dilemma of incompatibility with background theory of some current science. It is, indeed, a project that may need to be carried out before the major job of discovering the novel theory is fully taken in hand. This task is that of systematically reformulating the current theory in the hope of finding a version of it suitable for leading to its needed transformation.

Before exploring what such a project might amount to, it will be useful at this point to say something about a method often suggested for dealing with the issues that arise when a theory is found to be defective in one of the ways we have just noted. Quite correctly it is observed that the response to some anomaly confronting the theory, be it an empirical difficulty, an internally systematic problem, or some difficulty in reconciling the theory with the external theoretical background, may very well not be the flat-out rejection of the theory by the scientific community.

It is sometimes suggested that the proper way of understanding situations of this kind is to reject the idea that scientific theories, even foundational theories in physics, have pretensions to some sort of universality. Suppose we view theories as proposed ways of dealing with the world that carry with them implicit "ranges of applicability" or "spheres of legitimacy." We could then understand how a theory could be retained, and not rejected, even as its empirical or conceptual anomalies are baldly recognized and acknowledged. We can save the theory by just categorizing the places where the theory runs into empirical or conceptual difficulties as realms of phenomena excluded from the theory's implicit proper domain of applicability.

This view of theories as always limited in their pretensions of applicability is often yoked together with the claims we examined earlier to the effect that theories can only be rigorously true when they are applied to idealized situations that fail to match up with the way things are in the real world. That is, the idea of theories as never pretending to universality, but only to applicability in a limited domain, is often combined with the idea of theories as applying not to the world at all, but only to "models" that are similar to the world only to some degree and in some respects.

It is certainly reasonable to think of an older theory, once it has been replaced by a successor that is more empirically or conceptually adequate than it was or that has greater generality than it did, as living on in science in only such a domain-limited and approximative fashion. No doubt such a view of the present status of Newtonian mechanics in a world governed by relativistic and quantum theories does much justice to what scientists really think of as the remaining "truth" that the Newtonian theory can be said to possess. But to think of our theories in general in that manner is to miss a number of crucial points.

First, such a description of theories and the scientist's attitude toward them is untrue to the naive but real ambitions of science for genuinely universal and rigorously correct theories. Second, without great elaboration such an account of theories leaves almost all of the most interesting questions unanswered. One thing we would want to know is just how domains of applicability grow or shrink as the progress of science continually changes the status of some one theoretical account. Another thing we want to know are the details of just how it is that the theories genuinely apply to the real world for predictive and explanatory purposes. Merely to attribute to the scientist an attitude that implicitly takes the domain of any theory as restricted and its applicability as only indirect and mediated through models answers none of those questions.

More importantly, such a description of how scientists ought to view the status of their theories fails to attend to the rich field of investigation open to us when we explore the details of just how science goes about trying to fulfill its ambitions of universality and full rigor for its theories. Just how does theoretical science go about responding to the difficulties with current theories of the sorts itemized above? It is in trying to answer that question that the interesting insights are obtained.

4. RECONSTRUCTING THE PRESENT AS A GUIDE TO THE FUTURE

In the face of empirical and conceptual anomalies or failures of generality, just what cognitive attitudes toward our theories become possible and plausible? How do we fill in the schema that suggests that our attitude often becomes that of believing the theory to be pointing toward a correct future theory? What is the spectrum of methodological moves that can be made, here and now, to deal with the presence of anomalies or lack of desired generality? In particular, how are the choices of appropriate attitude, and the moves made to deal with the newly exposed problem areas, grounded in general methodological considerations, as well as in the contextually available scientific aspects of the problem situation?

There is a significant body of theoretical work in science that has been underexplored by methodologists. This is the work that often takes place in the light of the realization by the scientific community that the best available theory in some domain suffers from one or another of the defects noted above. Ideally, of course, the solution to any one of these difficulties is simply to come up with the new, improved theory that we are convinced will ultimately supplant our present problematic account of the world. But even if that future theory is presently unavailable to us, and even if the scientific community is quite uncertain about what such a future theory might look like in many important respects, the community is not therefore reduced to impotence and idleness. There are many important projects to be undertaken in lieu of what might be the currently impossible one of actually finding the desired replacement theory. These are tasks that, one hopes, will prepare the way for the arrival of the anticipated better account of the world. What are some of these tasks, and how might they be undertaken?

One thing that one can do with a theory when it confronts empirical or conceptual difficulties is to engage in a process of constantly recasting it in a wide variety of reformulations. By rearranging the theory's structural parts in numerous ways, and constantly reorganizing the theory in terms of a variety of possible alternative fundamental principles, one can hope to gain new insight into the internal structure of the theory. Such insight may be invaluable in suggesting directions in which the theory might be modified, changed, or generalized in order to deal with such difficulties as empirical anomalies, conceptual incoherencies, or failures of appropriate generality.

The realization that foundational theories in physics could appear in many quite distinct formal guises, invoking many different principles as fundamental and showing perspicuously quite different structural aspects, probably received its major impetus from the long history of the development of Newtonian mechanics from the seventeenth to the twentieth century. It may have been fortunate for physics that the Newtonian theory had such a very long run of success as the foundational theory of physics. This provided a long interval of time in which it could be discovered in just how many very different-looking formalizations a fundamental theory could be represented. The Newtonian theory can be presented in terms of forces that generate accelerations or that generate changes of momentum. The realization that there was a Least Action principle that paralleled the Least Time principle of optics allowed for the reformulation of the Newtonian theory as a generator of variational problems that takes the actual evolution of a system to be that evolution that gives the extreme value of a quantity, the action, over a possible dynamical path for the system from initial to final state, as compared with the value of that quantity when evaluated over those other dynamical paths the system does not take. This approach, as well as another that generalizes the principle of Virtual Work taken over from statics, leads to Lagrange's equations and the realization of the usefulness of introducing generalized coordinates, such as angle variables, and generalized notions of momentum conjugate to them, such as angular momentum, in describing the behavior of complex systems or systems whose evolution is subject to constraints. Later, a new formalization of the theory was discovered by Hamilton in the form of his paired, first-degree equations for the evolution of generalized position and momentum variables as controlled by the Hamiltonian energy function. Later still, a careful exploration of the ways in which a system whose description is framed in terms of one set of conjugate variables can also be described in terms of other sets of such variables, and of the rules for transforming the dynamics from one such description to another, led to reformulations of the theory in terms of Poisson brackets and in terms of the Hamilton-Jacobi equation. Finally, the theory has been recast in this century in a variety of formalisms of great abstractness and corresponding generality.

This wealth of variant reformulations and reconstructions of Newtonian theory was not developed originally because of any thoughts that the theory was defective in some way, nor with any primary sense of anticipating possible structures for some new, future replacement theory. Quite the contrary: it was because of the supreme confidence in the permanent status of the theory that so much effort was put into structuring it in such a variety of ways. The aim of the constant reconstruction of the theory was, in part, to understand the theory as thoroughly as possible, and, in part, to rearrange the theory continually so as to make its application to particular cases, constrained motion as well as unconstrained, motion of rigid bodies and of continua as well as of point particles, for example, as facile as possible.

The existence of this large class of reformulated versions of Newtonian theory, however, proved invaluable when the theory finally did encounter its empirical and conceptual anomalies and needed a replacement in the form of quantum mechanics. Wave mechanics has clear roots in Hamilton-Jacobi theory in which a pseudo-wave front in phase space characterized the trajectories of particles in classical mechanics. The construction of matrix mechanics, the alternative original formulation of quantum mechanics, made essential use of the formulation of the earlier theory in terms of Hamilton's equations. Later, when these two initial versions of quantum theory were assimilated into the transformation-theoretic approach of Dirac and the formulation of the theory in von Neumann in terms of Hilbert space, deep guidance toward the construction of the new version of quantum theory was provided by the representation of the Newtonian theory in its Poisson-bracket guise. This utilization of the manifold reformulations of the older theory to direct the construction of its replacement continued into the development of quantum field theory. In its initial version quantum field theory borrowed directly from the Lagrange-equation approach to the dynamics of fields in Newtonian theory. And later the path-integral version of quantum field theory was constructed by brilliant analogy with the principle of Least Action in the older theory and by extension from its variational methods.

There are other cases, though, where the motivation behind a program of constantly reconstructing or reformulating an existing theory was a direct attempt to prepare for a future as yet unknown. The theory of spacetime provides several illustrations of a kind of programmatic attempt to deal in the present with anomalies in current theory by reworking that theory in the hopes of gaining insights into how to replace it in the future.

Consider, for example, the need that was felt from the very earliest years of the existence of general relativity to generalize it in such a way as to encompass electromagnetism, then the other known fundamental interaction field besides gravity, in a dynamical geometric framework. This was the well-known program of Einstein and others of seeking for a unified field theory. The search for the generalization to the geometric theory of gravity took many different forms. One of these consisted in adding elements to the existing theory, such as the addition of a "compactified" dimension to spacetime in what became called Kaluza-Klein theory. But other approaches followed a route that beautifully illustrates our general theme.

General relativity was framed in the differential geometry of spacetime. But mathematicians had already begun the process of "picking differential geometry apart" even before differential geometry was applied to physical theory. A space or spacetime described by the full resources of differential geometry has an extremely rich mathematical structure. In the best mathematical tradition of abstraction and generalization, the questions had begun to be asked about how to distinguish each of the structural aspects of a space described by differential geometry from each of the other aspects. Such a space is, at one and the same time, a set of points describable in set theory; a continuum describable in topology; a differential manifold, that is to say, a space whose points can be referred to by a system of naming that utilizes a collection of co-ordinate systems each satisfactory over a sufficiently small patch of the space and smoothly related to one another where they overlap; a conformal structure, that is to say, one in which it makes sense to speak of the angles made by curves intersecting with one another at a point; a projective structure, that is to say, a structure possessing specially distinguished "least-curved" curves called geodesics; an affine structure, that is to say, a structure in which it makes sense to speak of "parallel transport" of vectors along arbitrary curves in the space; and, finally, a metric structure, in which it makes sense to ask of two points on a curve what the distance between them is along the curve. Mathematics had been systematically engaged in sorting out these structures from one another, characterizing them in terms of the essential elements needed for a structure of a given kind to be well-defined in a space, and asking such crucial questions as which structures were presupposed for defining which other structures.

The exploration of this rich mathematical structure, with its many layers of abstraction, and the disentangling of the various systematic components that went together to build up the full complexity of differential geometry, provided a number of suggestions for ways in which general relativity could be generalized by loosening the constraints placed upon one component or another within the existing theory.

Weyl, for example, noted that in general relativity a vector at a point that was pointing in some direction could be parallel transported around a closed loop, returning once again to the starting point. Intrinsic curvature of the spacetime revealed itself in holonomy, that is, in the fact that in general the vector when so transported would be pointing in a direction distinct from its original direction once the closed-loop transport had taken place. But in orthodox general relativity the length of the vector remained invariant under such transport. Could we not imagine a generalization of the theory, then, that would allow vectors to change their length upon such closed-loop travels? Just as change of direction revealed curvature, and hence, in the theory, the gravitational field in the region surrounded by the loop, could not the change of length be taken as the measure of the electromagnetic field through the surrounded region?

Einstein, on the other hand, noted that the mathematical connection, that mathematical device that characterized parallel transport in the theory, had a built-in property of symmetry in the orthodox theory. Cartan, however, had already explored a generalization of the kind of differential geometry used in general relativity that allowed for nonsymmetric connections. In the mathematician's terminology, the spacetime of general relativity was "torsion free," but spacetimes with nonzero torsion could easily be characterized. Perhaps the extra degrees of freedom allowed to the geometry by introducing nonsymmetric connections could provide just that additional mathematical richness needed to characterize the electromagnetic field.

Now it is the case that neither Weyl's gauge field theory nor Einstein's theory invoking torsion turned out to be the directions in which physics did, in fact, progress, although a radically modified version of the Weyl theory proved absolutely fundamental in a quite different context as the framework for so-called gauge field theories in quantum field theory. But the methodological insight holds nonetheless.

To sum up: Suppose one has recognized that a current theory

must be considered to be transient because it lacks appropriate generality. It hasn't run into empirical data that conflict with its predictions, and it hasn't displayed inner conceptual incoherence of some kind, but it has failed to characterize a part of nature that, it is felt, should be part of the domain of an integrated theory of which the current theory can be only a significant part. A reasonable methodological approach is to disentangle the elements that go to make up the full, rich theory. Then one can proceed systematically to explore the ways in which those elements function together to generate the full mathematical structure of the current theory. Next one can explore the more general structures that can be obtained by loosening the constraints imposed in the current theory on one or another of the components that goes to make up the theoretical framework.

There is, of course, no guarantee whatever that operating in this way will successfully allow one to discover the best novel theory to adopt that will satisfy the desire to find a theory that covers the domain that the current theory failed to handle. What is being suggested here is that in the face of our current belief about our present theory, that it is a theory not fully worthy of belief, but that it is a theory that points in the direction of where science is to go, we are led not to a quietism that simply awaits the arrival of the improved theory to which our current theory is directing us. There are systematic methods available that we can currently employ to explore possibilities for that future theory. And these methods are suggested by our very cognitive attitude toward the current theory, our belief, that is, that this theory, if not true, is at least pointing us in the direction of the truth. Indeed, it is our being disposed to employ these methods, I suggest, that is constitutive of what we mean by "believing the current theory to be pointing in the direction of the truth."

Spacetime theories can also be used to provide an example of a somewhat different way in which science can deal with a present theory acknowledged to be deficient, with the aim of anticipating a hoped-for better future theory. Consider the current attempts to try and reconcile the general relativistic theory of gravitation, framed completely in classical, nonquantum, terms, with the claim of quantum theory that its basic kinematic and dynamical characterization is universal in its application. It isn't only the claim of quantum mechanics to universality that is relevant here. There would be clear physical difficulties that would be encountered in any theoretical attempt to retain a nonquantum theory of gravitation in conjunction with a quantized theory of everything else. Here we have a clear example of one of the kinds of anomalies we noted above. It is not an empirical failure of general relativity that leads us to view its place in science as at best transient. Nor is it something internally incoherent in that theory that tells us that it cannot survive as our accepted theory in the long run. It is, rather, the inconsistency of the theory with an accepted background theory that leads to the refusal to accept the theory in question as the final truth or to unqualifiedly claim to believe it.

Trying to reconcile general relativity with quantum theory has proven frustratingly difficult. We cannot even begin here to look at the wealth of programs initiated to carry out the task, nor even touch on the manifold difficulties that they have run into. For our purposes I wish only to focus attention on the ways in which the continual exploration of and reformulation of the structure of the current, nonquantum, theory of gravitation has been undertaken in the hopes that such programs will aid in the search for the longed-for quantum theory of gravity.

We earlier noted one program for the reconstruction of general relativity. In this program the theory was presented on the basis of fundamental assumptions quite different from those implicit in the original, informal versions of the theory. The aim of that reconstruction of the theory, however, was not explicitly that of preparing the theory for future changes in the face of anomalies. The purpose, rather, was to unearth from within the theory a characterization of a possible "observation basis" for it that would invoke as its fundamental measuring devices only those entities whose physical behavior was characterized using the conceptual apparatus internal to the theory. For the purposes of "completing" the theory, that is, of framing the theory's account of measurement in terms internal to the theory itself, a formalization of the theory built up out of the observable behavior of light rays and free particles was deemed superior to a formalization where the observational consequences of the theory were characterized in terms of measuring rods (or tapes) and atomic clocks.

But in the reconstruction of general relativity that looks forward to the quantization of the theory, the search for observables appropriately internal to the theory is not what is at issue. Indeed, in some of the reconstructions proposed, it proves quite perplexing how to find the appropriate observational procedures with which to give empirical import to the entities and properties taken as basic in the reformulation. The aim of these new reconstructions of general relativity is to find a version of the theory that will prove less problematic than the standard versions when the task of "quantizing" the theory is undertaken.

Quantization is that process by which a classically formulated theory is transformed into a theory whose basic state variables and whose basic kinematics and dynamics follow the rules of quantum mechanics. Typically quantum theories are found by starting with a classical theory and making a number of transforming moves. The original quantum theory of particles is constructed, for example, by starting with classical dynamics with its generalized positions and momenta and exchanging operator-valued magnitudes for the classical-number-valued quantities. Sometimes finding the appropriate quantum surrogate for a classical theory is fairly straightforward, although there are usually problems of detail even in the simplest cases, since, for example, commutative quantities are being replaced by elements that do not commute. But in some cases, the prime example being gravity construed as the field theory in which spacetime itself is the field, finding the quantum surrogate for the classical theory is replete with difficulties. Some of these have the appearance of "technical" problems, for example, the fact that the usual methods of dealing with divergences in quantum field theory by renormalization fail in dealing with gravity.

But other problems can be much deeper. In quantum theories time usually plays a quite fundamental parametric role. But general relativity, with its dynamical spacetime and its general covariance, allows as legitimate any representation of events by means of a novel naming of events in spacetime coordinates. The very idea of what it would be to establish a quantization of spacetime itself requires deep conceptual rethinking of what our future theory is to be like. Much worse, the very possibility of formulating the principles usually taken as fundamental to any quantum field theory becomes deeply problematic in a spacetime itself taken to be subject to quantum fluctuational phenomena.

We noted above the way in which the many existing variations in the manner in which classical mechanics had been formulated provided many distinct routes into formulating quantum theory. For different purposes, different routes into the new theory proved more fruitful modes than did others. It was a major discovery, for example, that the quantum analog to the Least Action approach to mechanics, the method of path integrals, proved both an elegant and perspicuous way of representing the fundamental principles of quantum field theory, and a royal road to systematizing the terms of the perturbative expansions needed to calculate within that theory. On the other hand, for example, it was the Poisson bracket formulation of classical mechanics that provided the neatest route into understanding the fundamental role of the commutation relations in the algebraic foundations of quantum theory.

There are currently a number of programs that seek to reformulate general relativity in a wide variety of ways. Different objects and properties are taken as fundamental in these different reconstructions of the theory, and different lawlike constraints are taken as the axiomatic basis of the theory. All of these reconstructions are at least partially motivated by the hope that one formalization of the theory or another will provide some perspicuous route into the needed quantization of the theory. As an example of this approach, there is Ashtekar's proposal to formulate the theory in terms of holonomies, that is, in terms of the integration of its connection around closed loops. At the same time, it should be admitted that other approaches to a quantized theory of gravity follow other suggested courses, for example, trying to find the appropriate theory of quantized gravity as just one component of a general quantum theory of interaction fields. As an example of this approach, there is string theory in all of its manifestations.

Following out any of these examples, however sketchily, would clearly be impossible here, even were I qualified to outline their structural features intelligently. The point to be made, however, is a simple methodological one. When faced with the difficulty that our current best available theory is unbelievable because it is in deep conceptual conflict with the pervasive background physics that we accept, there is something we can do to deal with the situation that is preliminary to actually finding a more satisfactory theory to put in the place of our current best alternative. This is the systematic program of exploring the ways in which our current, unacceptable, theory can be reconstructed in forms that differ from its usual presentation. The aim of such reconstruction is to find a variant form of the current theory that is usefully suggestive in the overall program of science, namely, the program of finding the appropriate successor theory. Proceeding in this way, however, clearly indicates that although we believe the current theory to be at best a transient placeholder in the evolutionary progress of science, we also believe strongly that it does, indeed, point the way into the future. Were we to believe that there was no such value to our current theory, the program of ferreting out its many formal variants would seem entirely pointless in our endeavor to anticipate the future.

There is always the possibility, of course, that a program such as the one just described will fail to achieve its purpose. It may very well be the case that some imaginative leap, in a direction we cannot now even begin to contemplate, will provide us with the clues needed to come up with a theory of the world that does justice both to the facts accounted for in our current classical theory of gravitation and to those accounted for by quantum theory, but that bears no hereditary resemblance to one or both of our current theories. Such a theory, although it will have to do justice to the empirical adequacy of our current general relativistic theory of gravity, might deviate from the current theory so radically at its theoretical level that one would obtain no help whatever in discovering it by reflecting on the various ways in which the theoretical insights of general relativity might be construed.

The approach to a theory of quantized gravity through the theory of supersymmetric strings, for example, is one where the impetus toward the theory is only mildly guided by reflection on general relativity. Its main source of inspiration does, however, come from reflection on the structure of earlier theories of elementary particles. And even in this case some theoretical aspects of our best classical theory of gravitation are playing a role in constructing the newer theoretical possibility, for example, the fact that in general relativity gravity is a tensor field.

It also quite possible, of course, for a theoretical speculation generated in the ways we have been talking about to fail to come to fruition. Indeed, given the number of hypotheses that generally must be speculated about before the correct one is found, this is very likely. The attempts by both Weyl and Einstein at a unified field theory failed in their purpose. But the methodological points still hold. Within working science, theories are not taken to be merely temporary expedients solely because of some grand induction over the failure of the best available theories of the past. The grounds for skepticism with regard to their truth are, rather, specific empirical or theoretical difficulties faced by these theories. And the response of the scientific community to such difficulties with current theory can be systematic and methodical. It may include a program that is preliminary to the ultimate goal of finding a replacement that avoids the current theory's problematic aspects. Such a program may include the systematic exploration of the inner structure of current theory, possibly by multiple reconstructions in a variety of formal guises. Such reconstructions may be aimed at disentangling the various components that interact to form its complex theoretical apparatus, in the hope of finding some component of the overall structure whose constraints can be weakened in order to construct a more appropriately general theory. Or the reconstruction may be directed, rather, at finding a variety of different ways of presenting the theory as deriving from some set of chosen fundamental posits, in the hope that some one of these theoretical variants may be optimally suited for allowing an appropriate and needed transformation of the theory into one more compatible with the background science.

Both of these programmatic responses to the difficulties with the current theory presuppose that, defective as it may be empirically, internally, or in terms of its compatibility with background theory, it is the best guide available to us for searching out the future science to replace it. That is to say, such reconstructive programs implicitly assume that although we ought not to believe our current theory, we ought to believe that it points toward the future. Indeed, it is in unpacking the nature of such reconstructive programs that we begin to understand what we could mean when we claim that a theory is pointing the way to a more complete understanding of the world.

5. THEORIES ABOUT OUR THEORIES

General relativity suffers from an external conceptual incoherence. It fails to conform to the demands placed upon all physical theories by the background theory of quantum mechanics. Let us here explore an extended example of a case of internal incoherence. We have already noted a number of cases of internal incoherencies and of some responses to them. For example, one can sometimes deal with a conceptual difficulty internal to a theory by some kind of program of ontological elimination of some of the theory's artifacts at the theoretical level. Alternatively, one might attribute some internal conceptual difficulty to a failure to grasp the appropriate mathematics needed to present the theory in a manner that avoids its current internal difficulties. The difficulties encountered by Heaviside in using his ingenious operator methods found their solution in a rigorous theory of Fourier transforms; and it was discovered that the puzzles incurred by Dirac's invocation in early quantum theory of "functions" that were zero everywhere except at a point, but that had nonzero integrals, could be avoided either by using spectral decompositions of operators or by distribution theory.

Here, however, I want to focus on an ongoing program of a very different kind, a program designed to deal with a longstanding problem of internal incoherence in a fundamental theory. The program seeks a resolution of the problem by trying to understand, here and now, what the place of the present best available theory might be in some future science as yet unknown, afflicted with difficulties as that theory might be. This is a case where, once again, it can be argued that science progresses by exploring in depth the structure of a current theory, a theory that is acknowledged to be unsatisfactory in its present state. Once again, it is a case of believing the current theory to be pointing toward a better theory in the future. And it is, again, a case where a program is proposed that seeks to make progress by asking how the current theory might fit into a future science, even if that future science is as yet unknown to us. But it suggests carrying out this now familiar program by a method quite unlike those we have previously outlined. Here neither disentangling the components that make up the theory, nor seeking novel variants of its axiomatic formulation, will be our means of understanding how the current science points to the future. Rather, it is a *theory* about the present theory and its place in future science that is being proposed.

Quantum field theory can be thought of as having two origins. First, there was the need to apply to the classical field of electromagnetism the principles of quantization that had previously been applied to the dynamical states of particles. Second, there was the need to find a theory of particle interaction that allowed not only for changes in the dynamical states of particles, but also for the experimentally discovered possibility that particles could be created and destroyed. The theory resolving both of these problems was relativistic quantum field theory.

Some standard problems treated in that theory deal with the scattering of particles off one another. The dynamical interaction of the particles must allow for the possibility of particle creations and annihilations in the process of interaction. Exact solutions to a typical scattering problem are, however, usually out of the question. From its very beginnings the theory had, as an integral part of its structure, the construction of a number of approximation methods to be used to solve interaction problems. This perturbation theory looked toward the solution of any problem by means of the generation of a series of terms that took in successively more complex possible intermediate processes that could lead from an initial to a final dynamical particle state. The intermediate processes had to take account of the full realm of possible intermediate particle creations and annihilations that could serve to join together the initial and final states, even if such intermediate states were energetically unobtainable as genuine permanent states in the process. Finding systematic ways of generating such a series approximation, to serve as a representation of the perturbation theory, was a major accomplishment of the theory.

It was, however, afflicted with internal conceptual difficulties from its very beginnings. In particular, the terms in such a perturbation series could often be shown to be divergent, and in an infinite series, the series could be threatened by divergence even if all of its individual terms were finite. Computational results for such quantities as masses of particles, their charges, or the cross-sections (that is, the probabilities) for various dynamical transitions that resulted in divergent results were, of course, of no predictive use.

The appearance of such divergences was not entirely unexpected, since the classical theory of particles and their fields led to such unphysical divergences as well. As noted earlier (p. 100), the classical theory of electromagnetism treated the electron as a point entity, leading to the problem that it would interact with its own electric field whose magnitude diverged to infinite values at the point particle's location. Trying to get around this problem by treating the particles as extended led to many difficulties, such as accounting for their stability. The divergences of the new theory have an ancestry in the prequantum divergences, although in the new, much more complex account they present a far more intricate and subtle set of problems for the theory.

A number of methods were soon discovered for dealing with the divergences. They consisted in a variety of ways of "massaging" the theory in order to extract finite predictions from the divergent theory by systematically isolating the divergences and rendering them harmless. The finite values obtained, such as for subtle shifts in the energy level of electrons in atoms due to vacuum polarization effects, proved astonishingly accurate under experimental test.

The comprehensive study of such methods of keeping the divergences under control was called renormalization theory. Renormalization schemes eventually took on a wide variety of forms, some of them difficult to comprehend intuitively. The less intuitive programs, though, could be shown to be equivalent to methods whose intuitive basis was clearer. Perhaps the most intuitive, and most common, idea was to note that divergent results often occurred when all of the partial processes delineated by the terms of the perturbation series were added up to arbitrarily high energy levels. If one cut off the perturbation series at some finite energy, or, equivalently, thought of the possible interactions between the particles as being bounded below by finite spatial separations instead of being allowed to take place at arbitrarily close distances, the infinities might be made to disappear. But, alas, so would many desirable features of the theory such as the invariances demanded of it by relativity theory. Furthermore, the imposition of such a cutoff for the allowed energy of interaction would seem totally arbitrary unless it were justified by some further physical explanation.

But ingenious tricks were then discovered. One could introduce such a finite energy cutoff. Then one could rearrange the terms of the perturbation expansion in fruitful ways. After the rearrangement of terms, one could let the energy cutoff go back to infinity. The result would be, once again, divergences in the theory. But all of these divergences would be contained in the calculation of a finite number of observable parameters of the theory. In quantum electrodynamics, for example, the theory would calculate an infinite value for the mass and charge of the electron.

But then one could argue that the masses and charges of electrons measured in the laboratory were masses and charges that already had the divergent amounts contained in them. The "bare" mass and charge, parameters entering into the theory whose values were "corrected" in the divergent calculations of the renormalized perturbation series, were never open to experimental detection. One could, then, simply plug into the rearranged series the experimentally observed values for the mass and charge of the electron, essentially swallowing up all the divergent terms that appeared when the cutoff was allowed to go back to infinity. The new theory, without any remaining divergent terms in the series, could then be used to calculate finite correction terms that could be tested for accuracy in the laboratory.

Putting things so simply does little justice to the full complexity of renormalization theory. Renormalization schemes exist that do not use energy bounds. Dimensional regularization, for example, performs calculations in unrealistic spacetime dimensions, again rearranging terms, and finally bringing a dimensional parameter back to its natural value. Deep insights can be gained by reflecting on the way in which picking a specific value for the cutoff reveals its arbitrary nature. If one changes the value of the cutoff, various computed quantities change their values as well. But such changes of parameters may fail to show up in any changes in the theory's predicted values for observable quantities. The comprehensive theory of this phenomenon led to what is called renormalization group theory. This theory, in turn, proved of enormous value outside of quantum field theory. In particular, it led to a deep understanding of why it was that in the statistical mechanical theory of phase changes in materials, various features characterizing the phase change proved independent of many of the details of the substance undergoing the phase change, and dependent only on such general features as the dimensions of the system and the number of degrees of freedom allowed its components' microconstituents.

The methods of renormalization played an extremely curious role in the historical development of quantum field theory. On the one hand, the need for renormalization seemed to many a conceptually reprehensible aspect of the theory. It smelled to them of the *ad hoc*, and seemed lacking in the physical motivation and mathematical rigor that characterized the rest of the theory's formal apparatus. Much of the work in formal or axiomatic field theory, including that work that led to the local algebraic approach discussed earlier, was at least partly motivated by the desire to capture the portions of the standard quantum field theory that led to the correct physical predictions, while eschewing those parts of the theory that introduced the divergences of perturbation theory in the first place.

On the other hand, renormalization also became a criterion for when a proposed field theory could be considered a legitimate candidate for describing some aspect of the physical world. Not every kind of interaction is renormalizable. Renormalization requires that all the divergences that arise in the theory can be captured in some *finite* number of observable parameters in the theory. Here the divergences can be overridden in using the theory for prediction by substituting the observed values of those parameters for the "corrected bare values" that have turned out to be infinite. But most mathematically possible interactions do not lead to this option of swallowing all divergences into a finite number of such substitutions. The demand that a theory be renormalizable, then, serves as a severe constraint on the possible posited interactions allowed in a theory.

In addition, the theory that united the electromagnetic interactions with the weak interactions mediating beta decay of nucleons worked by imposing on an underlying symmetric dynamics a new interaction that broke the underlying symmetry of the interaction for the lowest energy states allowed in the theory. This is the famous idea of "spontaneous symmetry breaking." It was a major accomplishment to show that the special type of interaction proposed in this theory, a gauge interaction, remained renormalizable even in the face of spontaneous symmetry breaking. Only when this was shown was the new theory of the electro-weak interaction considered respectable.

The discomfort felt about the necessity for invoking renormalization methods, however, remained persistent. Attempting to bypass the formalism that gave rise to the divergences, and, hence, constructing a theory that would not require such seemingly *ad hoc* methods as renormalization, was one of the important motivations behind the program of axiomatic field theory. Perhaps rigorous postulates for the fields and the observables could be constructed that would allow the derivation of the desired field-theoretic results but would avoid some of the difficulties encountered in the informal development of the theory.

In Chapter 2, when discussing the topic of reforming theories by the process of ontological elimination, I noted that axiomatic field theory was itself afflicted with a number of difficulties such as Haag's Theorem and the problem of placing the theory in a curved spacetime background. I pointed out that one response to these problems was to try to move to a more "local" observation base for the theory. But in the construction of rigorous field theory there are, as we have noted, also moves that can be construed as moving away from concepts that are too local for their own good (see Chapter 1, section 4).

In much of axiomatic field theory it is assumed that talking about the values of fields at a point can only lead to difficulties. Some of the problems are mathematical, since the informal theory glibly allows for things, such as products of operators at points, whose mathematical rigor may be in question. But it is also reasonable to suppose that some of the divergence difficulties might have their origin in a too "pointwise" structuring of the theory as well. For this reason, axiomatic field theorists constructed systematic methods of dealing with observable quantities defined only over extended regions. In such an account the field values will relate to observables only when "smeared," by operating on functions that are nonzero only on compact regions and then by integrating the results. Here we have an approach to an internal conceptual difficulty that combines two of our earlier themes. First, there is an attempt to reconstruct a theory by restricting the ontology to the "real observables," here thought of as experimental determinations possible only over extended regions, such as detections of the presence of a particle within the nonzero volume of a Geiger counter's chamber. Second, there is the idea that the earlier version of the theory may have run into difficulties because of its overidealized form. By tolerating components of itself that refer to such idealizations as point values of field quantities, this informal theory may have ventured into nonempirical territory, thereby causing some of its conceptual difficulties such as the divergences.

Whether moves of this kind can really deal with the problem of the divergences is, however, not my concern here. Rather, quite another way of trying to deal with the divergence problem will illustrate my current methodological points. As field theory developed, and as new experimental data was accumulated, quite a new perspective on the renormalization problem became possible. This was the idea of an effective field theory.

Experiment showed that many "elementary" particles existed. Furthermore, these particles could be classified in hierarchies, characterized by families of particles of ever-increasing mass. It became apparent, when working out the details of interactions taking account of ever-greater numbers of ever-higher mass particles, that some divergences that appeared when higher mass particles were ignored would be "canceled out" when the additional particles were added to the calculations of the theory. Given such a hierarchy of particles, it also became reasonable to think of the older field theories, such as quantum electrodynamics, as only partial theories dealing with a limited domain of the phenomena. And their partialness here was of the sort that made attempts to use them to deal with their limited domain, as though that domain were not part of a larger world of entities and properties and as though the theory of those particles were not ultimately only part of a much more encompassing theory, potentially badly misleading.

These discoveries threw new light on an old debate. When the finite energy cutoff was first introduced as the means to renormalization, it was often viewed as reflecting a genuine failure of the field theory to function correctly at higher energies, and so as a means of dealing with a theory that was, at best, partial. Later, the general consensus seemed to be that the introduction of the cutoff had no such physical significance, but was only a formal device that succeeded, for reasons that were not totally clear, in allowing the generation of correct finite results by isolating the divergences. After all, it was sometimes argued, how could one take the cutoff as representing some real physical limit on the applicability of the theory, when the cutoff was always allowed to go back to infinity at the end of the renormalization process?

From the new perspective the cutoff of higher energies involved in the renormalization process could, once again, be thought of as something grounded in the real physics of the situation. It was not to be thought of as a mere formal device allowing regrouping of terms prior to abandoning the cutoff in the final stages of the calculation and then renormalizing the divergent parameters. The cutoff, rather, represented the limits on the domain of phenomena that could legitimately be dealt with by the lower energy theory. One could then think of quantum electrodynamics, say, as suitable for dealing with interactions in which the behavior of the higher mass particles was irrelevant. This means, of course, dealing only with the interactions of electrons and photons at sufficiently low energies, for at high enough energies the higher mass particles could then be created in the interaction, and their existence would constitute a significant factor in determining the interaction's parameters.

But we still want to know why the renormalization "gimmick" works. Even if including all of the higher mass particles there are might result in a theory without any divergences, the lower energy theory still has the divergences. Why does a theory with correct finite predictions result from the technique of introducing an energy cutoff, then rearranging all the terms in the series to group the divergent terms into a finite number of classes, and then letting the cutoff go to infinity but plugging in finite observed values for the parameters that ought, if calculated from the divergent classes of perturbation terms, to be infinite?

Responding to that question opens up a new way of looking at the conceptual problem introduced by renormalization. Suppose that one could characterize appropriate relationships that hold between the theory of elementary particles, that deals only with lower mass levels of the energy hierarchy of particles, and that fuller theory that encompasses in its calculations the particles in the next higher energy range as well: perhaps one could find in this special relationship between the narrower and the broader theories an explanation of why the narrower theory has the characteristics that it does have. This would involve explaining why the divergences appeared in the narrower theory in the first place, but also explaining why it is possible to deal with the divergences so successfully by means of the renormalization process. Such ideas are motivated by detailed calculations that show how, in particular cases, invoking higher mass particles in the theory can indeed eliminate some of the divergences that appear when these more energetic particles are ignored in the calculations.

What is remarkable is that it appears that just such relationships can be found. Interestingly, they can be characterized with some precision, even if one knows very little about just what the theory dealing with the particles at the higher energy range looks like in its detailed account of their interactions. The higher energy theory might not even be a standard quantum field theory of the same form as the lower energy theory. It might, for example, be a string theory in which the ordinary particles are treated as oscillatory states of a fundamental linear entity, rather than a point particle theory as is ordinary quantum field theory. The point is that even knowing very little about what the higher energy theory looks like, one may be able to postulate a structural relation among the theories as ordered into a hierarchy dealing with classes of particles falling into families of ever-higher energy range or mass. Such a "theory of theories" could then be used to explain many of the features of theories lower down the hierarchy as consequences of their very partial nature and of their place in the overall structure.

So-called effective field theories seek just such posited structures. They result in accounts that predict that the higher energy phenomena, phenomena that are neglected when partial theories dealing only with the lower mass particles are treated as standing on their own, will have serious impacts on the lower energy phenomena. But these impacts on the lower energy phenomena that come from the neglected higher energy realm can be categorized in deeply, systematically revealing ways. In particular, the neglected higher energy features of the world will have some impacts in the lower energy realm that are significant for experimental consequences there, but other influences on the lower energy phenomena that make only minor differences in the predicted behavior of things observed in low energy experiments.

The most astonishing results are those that then go on to give an account both of the divergences and of their renormalization. When the conditions demanded by effective field theory are met, the major impact of the neglected higher energy components on the low energy behavior of the low mass particles will be to introduce serious modifications in such parameters as the observed masses and charges of the lower energy particles. Renormalization deals with this by simply substituting in the isolated, partial, low energy theory the observed masses and charges whose value has taken the influence of the neglected high energy features into account.

But there will also be predicted non-normalizable effects on the lower energy realm coming from the neglected higher energy parts of the world. Given, once again, the conditions of effective field theory being met, these additional effects can be shown to be small. In particular, they will have their magnitudes proportional to appropriate functions of the ratios of the masses of the low mass particles to the higher mass particles. The greater the difference between the masses of the particles at the stage in the hierarchy above the one that the low energy theory is trying to account for, and the masses of those lower energy particles, the smaller will be the nonrenormalizable effects of the existence of the high energy realm on the low energy phenomena. It may be possible in some cases, however, to detect these effects that are neglected in the renormalized low energy theory. If there are phenomena that are totally excluded by the low energy theory because they violate some symmetry demand of that partial theory, and if the higher energy theory violates that symmetry, then some small nonrenormalizable effects at the low energy level may be detectable against the zero level of those effects predicted by the low energy partial theory.

Supposing effective field theory to be true, one can then speculate about the nature of the hierarchy of energy domains, and about the theories that belong to each level in that hierarchy. Perhaps the nature of the hierarchy is such that there is some "final theory of everything" that is fully consistent and has no divergences, and hence no need for renormalization. Perhaps the final theory is one that is itself divergent but fully renormalizable. (That option would puzzle us, for we would not be able to rationalize this last renormalization by appeal to further neglected domains of reality and their influence.) But, most enticingly perhaps, it may be that there is no "total" theory at all. Could the world be such that there is an infinite hierarchy of separated energy domains, with each such domain describable by a theory that is divergent but whose divergences are controllable by renormalization of a finite number of parameters? Each level could then display small nonrenormalizable effects not taken account of by the renormalizable theory of that level, but explicable as the result of the existence of the domain of phenomena at higher energy ranges.

It remains an open question at the present time whether the effective field theory approach will ultimately provide the framework for our expanding theory of the elementary particles. But the very possibility and the attractiveness of such an account to contemporary particle theorists usefully illustrates a number of the methodological issues that are our concern here. In the theory of elementary particles our current best available theory reveals itself as being afflicted with an internal conceptual difficulty: it is divergent. A series of approaches to reformulating the theory or "massaging" it in a number of distinct ways are designed that try to allow us to make successful use of our problematic theory despite its conceptual anomalies. These tricks allow us to make end runs around the apparent structural flaws in the theory. Despite the success of these methods, dissatisfaction remains due to the allegedly *ad hoc* nature of the manipulations of the theory, and due to the lack of any real physical understanding of the success of the methods. For this reason the theory remains in a state of limbo. It is neither fully believed nor straightforwardly asserted without qualification. Yet its striking empirical successes gain it a solid place in science for a long period of time, as it displays itself as by far the best available account that can be given of the phenomena in question. But hope abides all along that this disturbing account will prove to be only a transient way-station on the route to a theory that is equally empirically adequate but which is devoid of the present theory's conceptual anomalies.

One way to deal with such a problem situation, as we have seen, is to seek for reformulations of the theory that retain its empirical success but that seek the resolution of its internal conceptual difficulties in a mathematical restructuring that eliminates those artifacts that are inessential for its empirical success and that may generate its structural difficulties. A good part of the original motivation for axiomatic quantum field theory was founded, for example, on the hope that such moves as moving to rigorously defined "smeared" observables might remove the divergence problem from the theory.

Effective field theory, however, suggests a route out of the difficulties of quite a different sort. From this perspective, the difficulties of quantum electrodynamics that necessitated the need for renormalization are traced, not to mathematical artifacts in the representation of the theory, but, rather, to the theory's partial nature. It is because the theory tries to deal only with low energy phenomena in isolation, neglecting the higher energy features of the world to which the low energy systems treated by the theory are inevitably coupled, that the divergence problems arise. Looking at the current theory as a merely partial theory, that can be successfully understood only in the fuller context of the more general account of the world, provides a novel prospect for understanding both the origin of the divergences and the success of the renormalization method in inoculating the use of the theory from any damage caused by those infinities.

The treatment that effective field theory offers for this need to generalize the current theory provides an apt illustration of our general thesis that there are many things that one can do in science, here and now, to deal with the acknowledged temporary status of one's current best theory. Many of the things that one can do will not amount to fully displaying a better theory to take the place of the current, admittedly inadequate account. Effective field theory illustrates the possibility of developing an account of how our current best but inadequate theory may fit into a more adequate theory that, we hope, will be developed in the future. Such a theory about our current theory and about its domain of application can sometimes serve to explain the origin of our current best theory's problems, point to ways of fully resolving these problems, and even, in the case of renormalization, explain to us why temporary expedients can provide us with a way of legitimating and usefully applying our current inadequate theory by evading its inadequacies.

Effective field theory also illustrates the general thesis that one can well have a cognitive attitude toward current theory that amounts to believing that the current theory "points to a better future." Indeed, if we think of examples of the three modes we have explored for dealing with theories that are admittedly transient— disentangling their elements in the search for constraints to be generalized, rearranging their fundamental claims in the hope of finding a formulation suitable for appropriate transformation, and seeking for a theoretical understanding of the possible place of the current inadequate theory in some more general and more adequate account—we begin to understand just what the meaning of such a cognitive attitude might be. To believe a theory to be pointing to the future is to believe that the appropriate methodology for finding the way to some future, better alternative is the systematic exploration of the manifold aspects of the current, inadequate theory. We may not believe that we have the truth, but we often believe, and believe with very good reason, that the best way of getting closer to the truth is the systematic attempt to obtain a deeper understanding of what we do have, our best current theory to date, inadequate as that theory might be.

We might, of course, be wrong in believing the present best to be the guide to the better future. It might very well be that the history of science will be marked by revolutions so spectacular that they make our world picture entirely new, leaving us wondering how we had ever thought there was anything remotely right about what we had believed before the revolution took place. But claims to the effect that such revolutions have taken place in the past are, I submit, misreadings of even the most fundamental changes in our physical world picture to date. The belief that such radical conceptual revolutions will come about, or perhaps even be common, in the future, is itself a kind of skepticism that is, in some sense, impossible to refute. It is certainly difficult to imagine what such totally new world pictures might be like. They would at least have to preserve an understanding of why their predecessors worked empirically as well as they did.

There may be much to learn in examining the rational grounds that can be given for initiating one or another of the programs for exploring and reconstructing one's present inadequate theory with the intention of preparing for the future. It seems doubtful that we could formulate a "method of discovery" that would serve to guide us in any kind of determinate way as to how to carry out the program in a specific case. But there may very well be some general things to be said about how both wider methodological principles, and the scientific context of a specific problem situation, can make plausible one imagined program or another as the one best suited to the issues at hand. Such a "methodology of theoretical anticipation" might well supplement any methodology that proposes to offer insight into our grounds for justifying belief when a theory is actually at hand. We may very well have systematic ways of justifying one means or another of dealing with the structure of current theory, acknowledged as not worthy of belief. Here the justification would consist in plausibility arguments to the effect that some particular reformulative process applied to the present theory, or some particular way of theorizing about the current theory and its anticipated place in future theory, can be rationally argued for: it will be a reasonable scientific pursuit to follow given our general principles of methodology, the specifics of the difficulties encountered in the present theory, and the need to engage in some process or other of these ways of dealing with present theory seeing that we are unable to formulate now the better theory of the future.

Are there any other general insights that we can gain by looking at this last case of acknowledged transience of a theory due to internal conceptual anomaly and the attempt to deal with it short of finding the suitable theoretical replacement for that theory? I think that there are. I earlier noted the well-known proposal that we are to think of science as always proposing theories whose intended predictive and explanatory domains are to be thought of as, in principle, limited. It was argued by some of those who expounded such a view that the idea of science as seeking some universal theory that would encompass the full range of physical phenomena was delusive.

Here we are not dealing with the very plausible, but quite distinct, claim that even if some universal foundational physical theory were attainable, there would still be room in science for a variety of the "special sciences," each framed in its own concepts and each dealing with some special subsystem of the whole. The existence of a universal physics would, no doubt, leave room for biology and its subdisciplines and for social and psychological theories framed in their own vocabulary. The concepts of these theories would remain useful for sorting out the goings-on in their part of the world in ways not useful at all in the fundamental physics. Even a universal physical theory will allow us to continue to deal with the notion of a table or the notion of a biological species, for example. And there need not be any useful way, or perhaps any way at all, of defining what it is to be a table or what it is to be a biological species in terms of the concepts of the fundamental physics. What we are concerned with here, rather, is the claim that there could never be any such universal foundational physical theory at all.

I have argued that the limited domains of applicability of existing theories do not, of themselves, preclude as a realistic ideal the notion of some universal theory of the future, any more than the fact that these theories have in them, of necessity, many embedded idealizations makes them thinkable only as applicable to models and not to real systems themselves.

The case of effective field theory gives us an example that may throw some light on the issue of the claim of possible universality against the claim of the in-principle limited applicability of theories in general. For in effective field theory we see how the notion of theories as having at best limited domains of applicability, and the ambition of finding a theory properly claimed as universal, may be reconciled in a surprising and subtle manner. An essential part of effective field theory is the exploration of the extent of the domain to which a given quantum field theory can be applied with any expectation of predictive reliability. Another essential part of the theory is the exploration of how the limited domains of each field theory are related to one another and how these domains, and consequently their appropriate theories, are organized into a hierarchical structure. Effective field theory, then, might provide us with a new way of thinking about the possibilities of a universal theory. This would be so even if it turned out that there was no single "final theory" at the top of the hierarchy. Even if the hierarchy of theories went on forever, the description of that hierarchy itself would constitute, in a sense, a universalizing picture of the world.

What is especially novel about effective field theory is its claim that understanding how the individual field theories, each applicable only to its partial domain, fit into the overall universal picture, is absolutely essential for understanding the internal workings of each of the partial theories. For it is only by fitting the partial account into the global hierarchical picture that we understand the origin of the peculiar internal conceptual anomalies that afflicted each partial theory. And it is only by seeing the place of each partial theory in the hierarchical whole that we understand why the methods developed to work around these conceptual anomalies afflicting the partial theories were as successful as they were.

It is not yet clear whether or not effective field theory will itself become a permanent part of our accepted fundamental theory. But whether it turns out in the long run to be the correct way of dealing with the divergence and renormalization problems or not, its very existence as a hypothesis provides us with one more example of how working science can provide the methodologist with ways of thinking about the problems of method and of the structure of theories that would escape notice if they were pursued only from the abstract, science-independent perspective. Effective field theory shows us that there can be interesting alternatives to the view that theories will be, forever and in principle, domain-limited fragments that can be expected to deal adequately only with restricted portions of the world. But it is also an alternative to the simple view that there will be a universally applicable theory in the usual sense. It may turn out to be the case, for example, that fundamental physical theory will consist of an infinite hierarchy of theories, each dealing with its own limited domain, but all linked together by their place in the hierarchy. And, in addition to this, it may very well turn out to be the case that no one of the partial theories in the hierarchy can be properly understood in its internal features without making reference to its place in the overall structure.

What is being illustrated here could, I think, be illustrated by means of many earlier examples from the history of foundational physics. Our methodological insights must be continually refreshed and renovated by insights that can only be gathered by looking at the detailed workings of physical theorizing itself. That theorizing, which itself continually invokes philosophical modes of thought in its internal workings, also continually provides to the methodologists new ways of dealing with the world that carry in their specifics fresh ways of thinking abstractly about the possibilities for what a theory, a science, and a method might be or ought to be.

Suggested Readings

For general arguments against realism and the convergence of science to a unique, true description of the world see Kuhn (1970) and Feyerabend (1962). On subjective probability and action see chaps. 5 and 6 of Howson and Urbach (1993), and chaps. 2 and 3 of Skyrms (1984). For the connection of subjective probability to comparative believability see chap. III of Fine (1973), and Joyce (1998). Bayesian theories of scientific confirmation are discussed in part II of Howson and Urbach (1993), Earman (1992), and Maher (1993).

For constructive empiricism see van Fraassen (1980). For an account of scientific rationality that is "non-future looking" see Laudan (1977). Arguments in favor of convergent realism can be found in Boyd (1990) and his other works cited in that essay. Arguments against the comparability of theories differing radically in their portrayal of the world are in Kuhn (1970). For a Ramsey sentence approach to theory change see chap. VII of Sneed (1971). On "thinning content" to save a theory see Sklar (1985a).

For internal problems of quantum field theory see chap. II of Haag (1996). An introduction to the measurement problem in quantum mechanics can be found in Albert (1992), especially chap. 4. For the many varieties in which Newtonian dynamics can be formulated see Goldstein (1980). The ways in which quantum mechanics was initially developed using the various formulations of Newtonian theory as a guide are described in detail in Jammer (1966).

For unified field theories using Cartan's geometry in spacetime theory see Appendix II of Einstein (1950), and Cartan (1923). Weyl's gauge theory is in Weyl (1952). For some material on the problems encountered in trying to quantize the theory of general relativity see Isham (1991) and Ashtekar and Stachel (1991).

For a fundamental treatment of the mathematics used to make both Heaviside's operator calculus in classical physics and Dirac's delta functions in quantum mechanics mathematically respectable see Schwartz (1952). A brief survey of this work can be found in the Itô (1993) article 125, "Distributions and Hyperfunctions," in vol. 1, pp. 473–7, and article 306, "Operational Calculus," in vol. 2, pp. 1152–4. Further applications of this work are in Schwartz (1968).

For a brief and clear exposition of an alternative way of dealing with delta functions in quantum mechanics see chap. 3, sect. 17 of Jordan (1969). For a general discussion of some of the mathematical artifacts of quantum field theory and how to deal with them see Haag (1996).

For material on renormalization in quantum field theory see Brown (1993a), Dresden (1993), Mills (1993), and Shirkov (1993). For an introduction to renormalization in thermodynamics and statistical mechanics see Bruce and Wallace (1989). Introductions to effective field theory can be found in Georgi (1989), Cao (1993), and Schweber (1993).

5

Conclusions

We have been exploring three major grounds for being skeptical of the claim that our foundational physical theories are true. This skepticism amounts to denying the appropriateness of unqualifiedly asserting the theories and to denying the appropriateness of believing them. None of these philosophical critiques of a naive understanding of theories as purporting to assert truths find their motivation in an alleged arbitrariness or relativism in science and its methods of the sort currently so fashionable in today's descendants of some versions of pragmatism and of the sociology of knowledge.

There are three grounds for denying simple truth to theories we have been examining. First, there is skepticism with regard to those posits of our foundational physical theories that reach beyond the realm of the potentially observable, and which declare the existence and assert the nature of in-principle unobservable entities and properties. Second, there is skepticism that is directed at the claim that our theories can be taken as offering us true descriptions of the world and that rests upon the allegedly ineliminable need to resort to idealization in the formulation of our theories, idealization that would make our assertions true only of abstract models of things, if of anything, and not of things themselves. And, finally, there is skepticism regarding the naive assertability of theories that rests upon the claim that all of these theories are, at best, mere transient placeholders in our set of most esteemed hypotheses, and that each current favorite will eventually be replaced by some alternative account incompatible with it.

For each such variety of skepticism I have argued that there is a very rich set of methodological issues that are ripe for philosophical exploration and that have not yet received the attention they deserve. These are issues that only come to the fore when one realizes that considerations of ontological elimination based on epistemic critique, of the place of idealization in theory construction, and of critical response to the realization that a theory is merely transient, all play important roles within the ongoing process of science itself. In the construction of theories, in their critique within science, and in their reconstruction and reformulation as a scientific enterprise, each of the philosophical modes of skepticism generates its own specific, and often highly context-dependent, response in the form of specific modes of theorization within science.

I have no objection to treating any of the three skeptically motivated issues at the high level of abstraction with which they are usually dealt in methodological philosophy of science. I have no doubt that much has been learned, and that much more can be learned, of methodological, epistemological, metaphysical, and semantic importance when any one of the broad issues is treated in a manner that is as independent as possible of the specific details of particular theories within science. In particular, by dealing with these issues in such an abstract manner much can be learned about the deep connections implicit between the issues treated in methodological philosophy of science and those dealt with in general metaphysics, epistemology, and the philosophy of language.

But, I have argued, there is an entire realm of issues that are lost sight of unless we focus on the specifics of the ways in which critical philosophical modes of thinking play their roles within theory specific science itself.

Studying ontological elimination within science reveals to us the variety of specific and context dependent motives that lead science to propose programs that eliminate posited unobservable structures, programs that are partly argued for in epistemically rationalized terms. We see that the grounds for such programs are never mere positivist or empiricist considerations by themselves. It is some specific difficulty or another faced by a theory that leads the scientist to propose reforming it by removing some of its allegedly otiose unobservable elements. On the other hand, exploring the range of these detailed cases of ontological elimination in science reveals to us the fact that there are common roles played, across the many cases, by implicit philosophical concerns of just the sort that do motivate general empiricist and positivist philosophies. This last fact casts some doubt on the idea that one can view all of the methodological workings within scientific practice from a purely naturalistic perspective.

When the role of critical examination of the place of idealization in theories is looked at from the point of view of the role played by such critical analysis within science, one finds something quite different from what is emphasized by those who focus on the inelimin- ability of idealization from a more abstract perspective. Where the need for idealization becomes of real concern to the working scien- tist is not in those cases where some kind of "controllability" can be claimed for the idealization. The mere fact that the idealized assertions cannot be unqualifiedly taken to be true of real systems is not, by itself, a matter of grave concern. Nor is it counted as a deep matter that the idealized assertions might be thought of as unqualifiedly true only of some abstract model that is then related to the real world by some kind of similarity relationship, making the association of assertion to real world a two-step and indirect process.

We find, rather, that critical concern within science regarding the role played by idealization in our theories arises when deep theoret- ical issues of explanatory structure hinge upon the legitimacy of idealizations, a legitimacy that often cannot be decided one way or the other in any straightforward manner. In science, the legitimacy of treating a system as fully isolated from the world is truly a mat- ter of concern in such cases as the theories dealing with the origin of inertial forces, the theories dealing with the origin of temporal asymmetry in thermal processes, or the theories accounting for the special role of measurement in quantum mechanics. Here the issue is not the exact truth of some lawlike assertion that we might wish to make about the systems in question, but the very nature of the explanatory structure we are to posit for the phenomena in ques- tion. In science, the legitimacy of using some limiting procedure to obtain the needed results is of real concern only in such cases as statistical mechanics. Here, once again, the fact that limiting results can only be true of idealized models of real systems is not by itself a major cause for concern. It is, once again, the fact that different limiting procedures are employed as part and parcel of quite distinct attempts to offer grand theoretical explanations of the phenomena in question. Debates over the legitimacy of employing some limiting procedure, then, are really debates about which fundamental explanations are to be taken as truly accounting for what is to be explained.

When the issues in question are those raised by the alleged transience of theories in our accepted corpus of hypotheses, we find, once again, that the critical issues about transience that truly occupy the working scientists are quite different from those that attract our attention when some kind of methodological irrealism, based on the abstract consideration of the continual overthrowing of accepted theories, is in the forefront. Within science it is never the general possibility of a theory's being overthrown that leads to doubts about its truth. It is, rather, specific problems in the relation of theory to experimental data, or problems with theory's internal coherence, or problems in the theory's coherence with accepted background theory, that lead to the decision to view it as merely a transient placeholder and to the consequent critical discussion of it.

The response to skepticism induced by problems with the theory is rarely the simple adoption of a skeptical attitude toward the theory, or some wholesale rejection of it. The exposure of the difficulties leads more often, rather, to a motivated and systematic program of responding to the problems unearthed. What we have seen is that there are a number of recurrent structural elements that frame such responses. Further, the responses need not be immediate searches for the appropriate better theory to replace the theory in which the faults were found, but often constitute something preliminary for such a search. One can take apart the fundamental components of the theory in question and isolate the contribution of each part, hoping to localize the portion of the theory where the fault resides and make repairs in that specific portion. One can reformulate the problematic theory in a wide variety of ways, hoping that one of those reformulations will be ideally suited for suggesting what a replacement theory, freed from the flaws in question, might look like. Or one can develop a higher-level theory that studies how the problematic theory might fit in, as a partial account of the world, to a more complete overall theoretical structure, and how exploring this place of the problematic theory as partial might serve to allow the resolution of its apparent difficulties.

Each such mode of response to flaws in a theory constitutes part of a general program of "preparing for the future" when the present is found to be unsatisfactory. The fact that such a conservative mode of dealing with theories found inadequate—exploring and reconstructing them with a view to the future rather than simply tossing them on the rubbish heap of discarded theories—certainly suggests that claims as to the radicalness of even the most extremely revolutionary scientific changes, and claims about the alleged "incommensurability" of postrevolutionary theories with their predecessors, must be viewed with a great deal of reservation. Even if one doesn't believe in a theory one can believe that it points to the future. That amounts to treating with it in the ways we have noted.

The general moral to be drawn is that there is a profound role played within the scientific enterprise of constructing, testing and revising or replacing foundational physical theories by just the kind of critical, philosophical thinking familiar within general methodological programs. Scientific method is laden with philosophical methods and philosophical insights. But, at the same time, there is a rich store of methodological and philosophical understanding that can only be uncovered when the problems and issues familiar from general critical philosophy and methodology are explored as they arise within their context-dependent and theoretically and empirically motivated role, within the practice of science itself.

REFERENCES

ABRAHAM, R. and SHAW, C. 1992. *Dynamics: The Geometry of Behavior*. Redwood City: Addison-Wesley.

ABRAMS, M. 1971. *Natural Supernaturalism*. New York: Norton.

ALBERT, D. 1992. *Quantum Mechanics and Experience*. Cambridge, Mass.: Harvard University Press.

ASHTEKAR, A. and STACHEL, J. 1991. *Conceptual Problems of Quantum Gravity*. Boston: Birkhäuser.

BARBOUR, J. 1989. *Absolute or Relative Motion*, vol. 1, *The Discovery of Dynamics*. Cambridge: Cambridge University Press.

BATTERMAN, R. 1997. "In a Mist: Asymptotic Theories on a Caustic." *Studies in History and Philosophy of Modern Physics* 28B: 395–413.

BLATT, J. 1959. "An Alternative Approach to the Ergodic Problem." *Progress in Theoretical Physics* 22: 745–55.

BLOOR, D. 1991. *Knowledge and Social Imagery*, 2nd ed. Chicago: University of Chicago Press.

BOHM, D. and HILEY, B. 1993. *The Undivided Universe*. London: Routledge.

BOYD, R. 1990. "Realism, Approximate Truth and Philosophical Method." In C. Savage, ed., *Minnesota Studies in the Philosophy of Science*, vol. 14, *Scientific Theories*. Minneapolis: University of Minnesota Press: 333–91.

BROWN, L. 1993a. "Introduction: Renormalization 1930–1950." In Brown (1993b): 1–28.

—— ed. 1993b. *Renormalization: From Lorentz to Landau and Beyond*. New York: Springer.

BRUCE, A. and WALLACE, D. 1989. "Critical Point Phenomena: Universal Physics at Large Length Scales." In Davies (1989): 236–67.

CAO, T. 1993. "New Philosophy of Renormalization: From the Renormalization Group Equations to Effective Field Theory." In Brown (1993b): 87–134.

CARTAN, É. 1923. "Sur les variétés à connexion affine et la théorie de la relativité generalisée (première partie)." *Annales École Normale Superieure* 40: 325–412.

CARTWRIGHT, N. 1983. *How the Laws of Physics Lie*. Oxford: Oxford University Press.

DAVIES, P. 1989. *The New Physics*. Cambridge: Cambridge University Press.

DRESDEN, M. 1993. "Renormalization in Historical Perspective: The First Stage" In Brown (1993*b*): 29–56.

EARMAN, J. 1989. *World Enough and Space-Time*. Cambridge, Mass.: MIT Press.

—— 1992. *Bayes or Bust: A Critical Examination of Bayesian Confirmation Theory*. Cambridge, Mass.: MIT Press.

EHLERS, J., PIRANI, F., and SCHILD, A. 1972. "The Geometry of Free Fall and Light Propagation." In L. O'Raifeartaigh, ed. *General Relativity*. Oxford: Clarendon Press: 63–84.

EINSTEIN, A. 1950. *The Meaning of Relativity*. Princeton: Princeton University Press.

FEYERABEND, P. 1962. "Explanation, Reduction, and Empiricism." In H. Feigl and G. Maxwell, eds., *Minnesota Studies in the Philosophy of Science*, vol. 3, *Scientific Explanation, Space, and Time*. Minneapolis: University of Minnesota Press: 28–97.

FINE, T. 1973. *Theories of Probability: An Examination of Foundations*. New York: Academic Press.

FRIEDMAN, M. 1983. *Foundations of Space-Time Theories: Relativistic Physics and Philosophy of Science*. Princeton: Princeton University Press.

GAMBINI, R. and PULLIN, J., eds. 1996. *Loops, Knots, Gauge Theories and Quantum Gravity*. Cambridge: Cambridge University Press.

GEORGI, H. 1989. "Effective Field Theories." In Davies (1989): 425–45.

GIERE, R. 1988. *Explaining Science: A Cognitive Approach*. Chicago: University of Chicago Press.

GOLDSTEIN, H. 1980. *Classical Dynamics*, 2nd ed. Reading, Mass.: Addison-Wesley.

HAAG, R. 1996. *Local Quantum Physics: Fields, Particles, Algebras*, 2nd ed. Berlin: Springer.

HANSON, N. 1958. *Patterns of Discovery*. Cambridge: Cambridge University Press.

HEMPEL, C. 1965. "The Theoretician's Dilemma." In C. Hempel, *Aspects of Scientific Explanation and Other Essays in the Philosophy of Science*. New York: Free Press: 173–228.

HENNEAUX, M. and TEITELBOIM, C. 1992. *Quantization of Gauge Systems*. Princeton: Princeton University Press.

HESSE, M. 1966. *Models and Analogies in Science*. Notre Dame, Ind.: University of Notre Dame Press.

HORWICH, P. 1987. *Asymmetries in Time*. Cambridge, Mass.: MIT Press.

HOWSON, C. and URBACH, P. 1993. *Scientific Reasoning: The Bayesian Approach*, 2nd ed. Chicago: Open Court.

ISHAM, C. 1991. "Conceptual and Geometrical Problems in Quantum Gravity." In H. Mitter and H. Gausterer, eds., *Recent Aspects of Quantum Fields*. New York: Springer: 123–229.

ITÖ, K., ed. 1993. *Encyclopedic Dictionary of Mathematics*, 2nd ed. Cambridge, Mass.: MIT Press.

JAMMER, M. 1966. *The Development of Quantum Mechanics*. New York: McGraw-Hill.

—— 1974. *The Philosophy of Quantum Mechanics: The Interpretations of Quantum Mechanics in Historical Perspective*. New York: Wiley.

JORDAN, T. 1969. *Linear Operators for Quantum Mechanics*. New York: Wiley.

JOYCE, J. 1998. "A Nonpragmatic Vindication of Probabilism." *Philosophy of Science* 65: 575–603.

KOPERSKI, J. 1998. "Models, Confirmation, and Chaos." *Philosophy of Science* 65: 624–48.

KUHN, T. 1970. *The Structure of Scientific Revolutions*, 2nd ed. Chicago: University of Chicago Press.

LANFORD, O. 1983. "On a Derivation of the Boltzmann Equation." In J. Lebowitz and E. Montroll, eds., *Non-Equilibrium Phenomena I: The Boltzmann Equation*. Amsterdam: North-Holland.

LAUDAN, L. 1977. *Progress and its Problems*. Berkeley: University of California Press.

LAYMON, R. 1985. "Idealization and the Testing of Theory by Experimentation." In P. Achinstein and O. Hannaway, eds., *Observation, Experimentation and Hypothesis in Modern Physical Science*. Cambridge, Mass.: MIT Press: 147–73.

LEBOWITZ, J. 1983. "Microscopic Dynamics and Macroscopic Laws." In C. Horton, L. Reichl, and V. Szebehely, eds., *Long-Time Prediction in Dynamics*. New York: Wiley.

MAHER, P. 1993. *Betting on Theories*. Cambridge: Cambridge University Press.

MALAMENT, D. 1986. "Newtonian Gravity, Limits, and the Geometry of Space." In R. Colodny, ed. *From Quarks to Quasars: Philosophical Problems of Modern Physics*. Pittsburgh: University of Pittsburgh Press: 181–201.

MARZKE, R. and WHEELER, J. 1964. "Gravitation as Geometry, I: The Geometry of Spacetime and the Geometrodynamical Standard." In H.

146   *References*

Chiu and W. Hoffman, eds., *Gravitation and Geometry*. New York: Benjamin: 40–64.

MAYER, J. 1961. "Approach to Thermodynamic Equilibrium." *Journal of Chemical Physics* 34: 1207–20.

MAXWELL, G. 1962. "The Ontological Status of Theoretical Entities." In H. Feigl and G. Maxwell, eds., *Minnesota Studies in the Philosophy of Science*, vol. 3, *Scientific Explanation, Space, and Time*. Minneapolis: University of Minnesota Press: 3–27.

MILLS, R. 1993. "Tutorial on Infinities." In Brown (1993*b*): 57–86.

OMNÈS, R. 1994. *The Interpretation of Quantum Mechanics*. Princeton: Princeton University Press.

OZORIO DE ALMEIDA, A. 1988. *Hamiltonian Systems: Chaos and Quantization*. Cambridge: Cambridge University Press.

PETERSEN, A. 1968. *Quantum Physics and the Philosophical Tradition*. Cambridge, Mass.: MIT Press.

PICKERING, A. 1984. *Constructing Quarks*. Chicago: University of Chicago Press.

POLANYI, M. 1958. *Personal Knowledge: Towards a Post-Critical Philosophy*. London: Routledge & Kegan Paul.

PUTNAM, H. 1978. "Realism and Reason." In H. Putnam, *Meaning and the Moral Sciences*. London: Routledge.

—— 1990. "A Defense of Internal Realism." In H. Putnam, *Realism With a Human Face*. Cambridge, Mass.: Harvard University Press.

QUINE, W. 1969. "Epistemology Naturalized." In W. Quine, *Ontological Relativity and Other Essays*. New York: Columbia University Press.

—— 1990. *Pursuit of Truth*. Cambridge, Mass.: Harvard University Press.

RAMSEY, F. 1960. "General Propositions and Causality." In F. Ramsey, *The Foundations of Mathematics*. Paterson, N.J.: Littlefield, Adams.

REDHEAD, M. 1980. "Models in Physics." *British Journal for the Philosophy of Science* 31: 154–63.

ROHRLICH, F. 1989. "The Logic of Reduction: The Case of Gravitation." *Foundations of Physics* 19: 1151–70.

—— 1990. "There is Good Physics in Reduction." *Foundations of Physics* 20: 1399–1412.

RUELLE, D. 1969. *Statistical Mechanics*. New York: Benjamin.

RYDER, L. 1985. *Quantum Field Theory*. Cambridge: Cambridge University Press.

RYLE, G. 1950. "'If,' 'So,' and 'Because.'" In M. Black, ed., *Philosophical Analysis: A Collection of Essays*. Ithaca: Cornell University Press.

SCHWARTZ, L. 1952. *Introduction to the Theory of Distributions*. Toronto:

University of Toronto Press.

—— 1968. *Application of Distributions to the Theory of Elementary Particles in Quantum Mechanics*. New York: Gordon & Breach.

SCHWEBER, S. 1993. "Changing Conceptualization of Renormalization Theory." In Brown (1993b): 135–66.

SHIRKOV, D. 1993. "Historical Remarks on the Renormalization Group." In Brown (1993b): 167–86.

SKLAR, L. 1974. *Space, Time and Spacetime*. Berkeley: University of California Press.

—— 1985a. "Do Unborn Hypotheses Have Rights?" In Sklar (1985c): 148–66.

—— 1985b. "Facts, Conventions and Assumptions in the Theory of Spacetime." In Sklar (1985c): 73–147.

—— 1985c. *Philosophy and Spacetime Physics*. Berkeley: University of California Press.

—— 1993. *Physics and Chance: Philosophical Issues in the Foundations of Statistical Mechanics*. Cambridge: Cambridge University Press.

SKYRMS, B. 1984. *Pragmatics and Empiricism*. New Haven: Yale University Press.

SMITH, P. 1998. *Explaining Chaos*. Cambridge: Cambridge University Press.

SNEED, J. 1971. *The Logical Structure of Mathematical Physics*. New York: Humanities Press.

STREATER, R. and WIGHTMAN, A. 1964. *PCT, Spin, Statistics and All That*. New York: Benjamin.

VAN FRAASSEN, B. 1980. *The Scientific Image*. Oxford: Clarendon Press.

VISCONTI, A. 1969. *Quantum Field Theory*. Oxford: Pergamon.

WALD, R. 1994. *Quantum Field Theory in Curved Spacetime and Black Hole Thermodynamics*. Chicago: University of Chicago Press.

WEINBERG, S. 1995. *The Quantum Theory of Fields*, vol. 1. Cambridge: Cambridge University Press.

WEYL, H. 1952. *Space-Time-Matter*.

INDEX